Government Street

Government Street

VICTORIA'S HERITAGE MILE

Danda Humphreys

VICTORIA · VANCOUVER · CALGARY

Heritage House Publishing Company Ltd.
heritagehouse.ca

LIBRARY AND ARCHIVES CANADA CATALOGUING IN PUBLICATION

Humphreys, Danda

   Government Street: Victoria's heritage mile / Danda Humphreys.
ISBN 978-1-927051-38-2

   1. Government Street (Victoria, B.C.)—History. 2. Victoria (B.C.)—Buildings, structures, etc.—History. 3. Historic buildings—British Columbia—Victoria. I. Title.

FC3846.67.H84 2012   971.1'28   C2012-901018-9

Edited by Audrey McClellan
Proofread by Karla Decker
Cover and book design by Jacqui Thomas
Front cover: Looking north on Government Street *circa* 1940, postcard courtesy of Robert Battcchio; top photos by Rodger Touchie (first and fifth from left), Danda Humphreys (third and fourth) and John Walls (second, sixth and seventh)
Frontispiece: Looking south on Government Street in the early 1900s; the view is dominated by the old post office (long since demolished) on the right. Postcard from Heritage House collection.

 This book was produced using FSC®-certified, acid-free paper, processed chlorine free and printed with vegetable-based inks

Heritage House acknowledges the financial support for its publishing program from the Government of Canada through the Canada Book Fund (CBF), Canada Council for the Arts and the province of British Columbia through the British Columbia Arts Council and the Book Publishing Tax Credit.

16 15 14 13 12 1 2 3 4 5

Printed in Canada

For J.

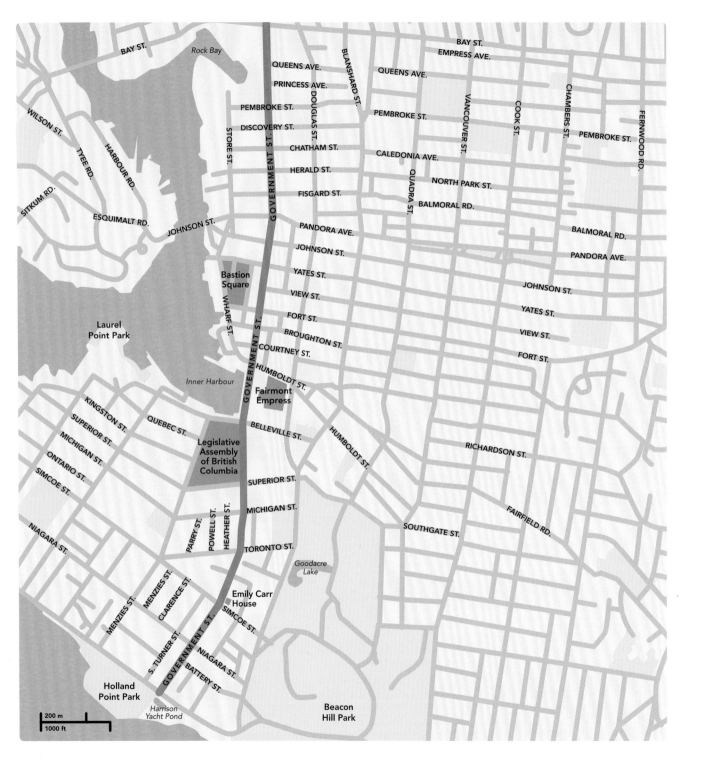

Contents

Introduction

For over 160 years, Government Street has carved a path through Victoria's history. Not so long ago it was just a dirt track beside a fur-trading post. Before that it was the traditional home of the Lekwungen and Songhees people, members of a larger group known as the Coast Salish, who for centuries had overwintered around the harbour.

Government Street, which once formed the eastern perimeter of Fort Victoria, was named because Government House stood opposite the fort's back gate. This is where Richard Blanshard, first governor of Vancouver Island, lived and worked.

Blanshard's appointment was a disappointment to James Douglas, chief factor at the nearby fort. A decade earlier, Douglas had chosen this site for a Hudson's Bay Company operation. Knowing the fort was destined to be the London-based company's headquarters on the west coast, he had named it Fort Victoria after the young British queen of the day—and he had fully expected to be the man in charge.

The British government, however, had other ideas. Leasing Vancouver Island to the HBC and holding Douglas responsible for settling it "in the British style" had seemed like a good idea at the time. But now parliamentarians were not convinced that having one man act both as chief factor for the HBC and as governor of the new Crown colony was serving their best interests.

Dismayed by their decision, Douglas declined to make their new appointee welcome. He provided only minimal support. And when he finally saw fit to spare the carpenters to work on the governor's residence, the plans only allowed for a small, bleak, barely appropriate "Government House" opposite the fort's back gate.

Douglas's less-than-friendly efforts bore fruit. The hapless Blanshard sailed out of Victoria's harbour in 1851, just 18 miserable months after he had sailed into it, and Douglas became governor after all.

Seven years later, life at the HBC's Pacific Northwest headquarters was disrupted by the discovery of gold on the mainland. Fort Victoria became the jumping-off point for the goldfields. The first boatload of gold seekers, who sailed into our harbour on April 20, 1858, doubled the 300-strong population in one day. Within a few months, 30,000 people had come from far and wide. Many went straight to the goldfields; others stayed to mine the miners—selling food and supplies for their forays to the Fraser River, ready to provide goods and services in exchange for gold dust when they returned.

In no time at all, the settlement became a small town full of people with big ambitions. In 1860, with fur sales dwindling, the HBC ordered Douglas to demolish the fort and sell the land. Meanwhile, eager entrepreneurs set up shop wherever they could find space. Before long, Government Street was lined with providers—a plethora of grocers and provisioners, butchers, bakers, cabinetmakers, saloon keepers and more—competing with each other for business along both sides of the dirt track that some hoped would soon be paved with gold.

In 1862, Victoria became a city. Two years later the fort was gone, its footprint filled with commercial structures. In 1868, Victoria was named the capital of the Crown colony of British Columbia, formed by the merger of colonies on Vancouver Island and the mainland. Three years later, the colony became a province. We were now part of the Dominion of Canada. The city's future seemed assured.

By 1881, Victoria's population had increased to 6,000. Ten years later the population stood at just under 17,000. The city's fortunes, which had waxed and waned over the decades, revived in the late 1890s when a new generation of gold diggers came through on their way to the Klondike. Optimism was in the air. The pioneering days were over. A new century had begun.

No one could have guessed what was in store. Victoria's fortunes fluctuated wildly as two major fires three years apart decimated parts of downtown, and a Depression, sandwiched between two world wars, changed the face of Government Street. In the 1960s, an attempt to boost the city's fortunes resulted in a major push for modernization and redevelopment. Concerned citizens rallied to protect our heritage. Thanks to them, most of our original downtown structures have survived, looking much as they did in days gone by.

In 2012—Victoria's 150th year as a city—Government Street remains a focal point. From Chinatown to Dallas Road, the street is a study in contrasts. In these pages you'll discover fascinating facts, turn historic corners and meet some of the colourful characters who made their mark along, and beyond, Victoria's Heritage Mile.

Government Street A TIMELINE

1500 Greek navigator Apóstolos Valerianos, who preferred the name Juan de Fuca, sails into the waterway that lies at the south end of Government Street.

1843 James Douglas and 19 men sail into Victoria's harbour to build a Hudson's Bay Company fort on the traditional land of the Lekwungen.

1849 Vancouver's Island, a Crown colony named after famed explorer George Vancouver, is created.

1850 Richard Blanshard, appointed by the British government to be the first governor of Vancouver's Island, arrives at Fort Victoria.

1851 Blanshard resigns and sails back to England. Douglas is named governor.

1852 Joseph Pemberton lays out the townsite. Its boundaries are the harbour and today's Broughton, Government and Johnson Streets.

1858 Gold rush! First of thousands of gold miners arrive. Chinatown established. Mainland becomes the Colony of British Columbia.

1860 First colonial administration buildings, known as "The Birdcages," officially opens at the south end of the new James Bay Bridge.

1862 Victoria (population 600) is incorporated as a city. Thomas Harris is first mayor.

1864 Demolition of Fort Victoria buildings, stockades and bastions complete.

1868 Island and mainland colonies combine to become British Columbia. Victoria declared the capital.

1869 Second James Bay Bridge constructed. First bicycles appear on Government Street.

1871 British Columbia becomes sixth province to join Canadian Confederation.

1881 Victoria's population is just under 6,000.

1886 Population: 11,401—8,400 whites, 2,900 Chinese, 101 Aboriginals.

Canadian Pacific Railway's western terminus, the village of Granville, is renamed "Vancouver" after George Vancouver.

1888	First Esquimalt & Nanaimo Railway train steams across the Johnson Street Bridge.	**1916**	Army called out to clear downtown streets after major snowfall.
1890	Streetcar service officially starts.	**1917**	Prohibition begins (1917–21). Government Street saloons feel the pinch.
1891	Population: 16,841. Downtown Victoria boasts 55 hotels and taverns.	**1922**	Traffic on Government Street starts driving on the right.
1892	Port of Victoria closed by smallpox epidemic.	**1931**	Population: 39,082.
1894	First "motor carriages" appear on Government Street.	**1937**	Hanging flower baskets introduced to celebrate city's 75th birthday.
1898	New British Columbia Legislative Buildings completed.	**1951**	Population: 51,331.
1901	Queen Victoria dies in England. City goes into mourning.	**1957**	Last of "The Birdcages" destroyed by fire.
1901	Population: 21,000. Ninety-five percent of Canada's Chinese now live in Victoria's Chinatown.	**1962**	City celebrates its 100th birthday.
		1965	Official opening of Centennial Square.
1907	Major fire destroys most of Chinatown.	**1968**	Provincial museum opens. Downtown streets become one-way.
1909	First Chinese public school in Canada opens in Chinatown.	**1967**	Chinese finally given full rights of citizenship.
1910	Major fire destroys the Five Sisters Block, David Spencer's Arcade and several other Government Street buildings.	**1973**	City appoints first Heritage Advisory Committee. Citizens form Hallmark Society.
		1976	Population: 62,552.

1977 Government Street's "heritage mile" becomes "heritage kilometre."

1983 City establishes Victoria Heritage Foundation and Heritage Trust.

1985 Gretchen Brewin elected Victoria's first woman mayor.

1990 Eaton Centre opens on Government Street.

1991 Population: 67,380. Empress Hotel featured on a Canadian postage stamp.

1991 Victoria hosts Commonwealth Games. Harbourfest a huge success.

1996 The heaviest snowfall since 1916 makes Government Street impassable.

1998 Hundredth anniversary of the opening of the BC Legislative Buildings.

2012 Victoria celebrates its 150th year as a city. Population nears 100,000.

Greater Victoria population is more than 338,000.

Starting Point
FORT AND GOVERNMENT
Crossroads of History

At the intersection of Fort and Government, take a deep breath and look around. You're standing at the crossroads of history. This is where Victoria began!

Back in the 1840s, you'd have been standing on the east side of Fort Victoria. It was the Hudson's Bay Company's latest venture—a new Pacific Northwest headquarters in British territory, north of the 49th parallel. From here to the harbour, Fort Street was the wide track between the fort's east gate on Government Street and its west gate on the waterfront.

The plaques on the building at this intersection's southwest corner tell us that the fort was here, and circular brass markers in the sidewalk mark the location of the back gate, where HBC workers and their families started on their journey to a new, independent life. Hundreds of thousands of gold seekers passed through this gate too, along with the merchants who sought to serve them.

Whether you choose to walk north from here, or south, you'll be following in the footsteps of some of those early arrivals, finding out where they came from, what brought them here and how we remember them in the city that we see today.

❧ TOUR 1 ❧ NORTH FROM FORT

J.J. SOUTHGATE'S BUILDING
1102 Government at Fort

It's been more than 150 years since James Johnson Southgate first stood where you're standing today. Then, he was one of a group of concerned citizens at the Fort Victoria compound petitioning Governor James Douglas for a fire department. Ten years later, this was the site of his business premises. The fort was gone. Douglas had retired in 1864, and Southgate was a force to be reckoned with on the local business and political scene.

PEMBROKE

DISCOVERY

CHATHAM

HERALD ST

FISGARD

PANDORA

JOHNSON

YATES ST.

VIEW

FORT ST.

BROUGHTON

COURTNEY

HUMBOLDT

Fairmont
Empress

BELLEVILLE

SUPERIOR

MICHIGAN

TORONTO ST

SIMCOE ST.

Southgate arrived here in 1859, when the gold rush was in full swing. He was a retired English sea captain, now more inclined to stay on dry land. While most of the men on his ship from San Francisco headed to the mainland to dig for gold, Southgate set himself up as a wholesale commission merchant. He took a keen interest in public affairs, becoming the Salt Spring Island member of the legislative assembly, first chair of the newly formed chamber of commerce, and the newly chartered Masonic Lodge's first Worshipful Master.

⌘ As we look north along Government Street around 1900, a streetcar waits for this well-dressed trio to cross the intersection before turning up Fort Street. Southgate and Lascelles' building stands at left, close to the former site of the fort's mess hall. Note the store owners' thoughtfulness in providing awnings to protect their goods from sun and their customers from rain. On the right in the picture is the Five Sisters Block, containing offices for barristers and architects, including Francis Rattenbury and Samuel Maclure. Beyond it is David Spencer's Arcade and other businesses on the main floor, with offices for barristers and architects, including Francis Rattenbury and Samuel Maclure, on the upper level. Today, the street has been narrowed to make more room for pedestrians, and trees provide much-needed shade. A microwave tower on the Southgate building's roof marks the location of Fort Victoria's bell tower. The Bay Centre now stands on the right.

PEMBROKE

DISCOVERY

CHATHAM S

HERALD ST

FISGARD S

PANDORA A

JOHNSON S

YATES ST.

VIEW

FORT ST.

BROUGHTON

COURTNEY S

HUMBOLDT S

Fairmon
Empres

BELLEVILLE

SUPERIOR S

MICHIGAN

TORONTO S

SIMCOE ST.

On a trip to France in 1867, Southgate met an old friend, the Honourable Horace Douglas Lascelles of the Royal Navy. The two sailed back here together in 1868. The following year they invested in a piece of prime downtown real estate and erected two handsome brick stores on the corner of Government and Fort. Their single-storey brick building, adorned with cast iron, had large windows facing onto street-level verandahs. Soon a second floor was added, its distinctive tall windows topped with sharply arched pediments.

Lascelles was long since buried in the naval cemetery at Esquimalt by the time Southgate returned to England, where he died in 1894. All that's left to remind us of these two enterprising businessmen is the building where they made their mark. And the building itself bears an intriguing reminder of the simple, stockaded structure that once stood on this site.

If you stand on the Fort Street side and look up, you'll see the microwave tower, designed to resemble a campanile, on the same spot once occupied by Fort Victoria's bell tower. Over 150 years ago the bell clanged greetings, warnings and congratulations. Today it stands as a mute reminder of Victoria's fur-trade beginnings and of the two men who conducted business on this corner many, many decades ago.

⌘ Looking down Fort Street toward the harbour, you'd swear someone was smiling at you from an upper window on Langley Street. Get a little closer, and you'll see that the side of the Siam Thai Restaurant (512 Fort) sports Jeff and Trudy Maltby's eye-catching murals. While reading the description underneath, look to the right and you'll see Frank Lewis's mural "Time Steps" on the side wall of the Luxe Building at 1114 Langley Street. If you had stood here in the days of Fort Victoria, you would have been surrounded by HBC residences, a school, mess hall, fur-trading store, and warehouses full of beaver and otter pelts.

THE BAY CENTRE
1100-block Government

Across the street from Southgate's building, the Bay Centre looks way too modern to be part of old Victoria. In fact, this building, which replaced several early structures, dates from 1990. And it caused a fair amount of controversy at the time.

Toward the end of the 1980s, Toronto-based real estate giant Cadillac Fairview announced its plans to create a major shopping mall on Government Street in partnership with the T.E. Eaton Company. When it became apparent that almost a dozen heritage structures dating from the 1880s through the 1920s would be demolished to make way for the new mall, local citizens were understandably upset.

Feeling the pressure, Cadillac Fairview agreed to reconstruct the facades of the buildings concerned. By Christmas 1986 the city had given its blessing to the $1-million development. The old buildings disappeared in a huge pile of rubble. However, the original bricks did not meet modern building code standards, so the facades were constructed using new materials. By 1990 the new structure reigned supreme.

The T.E. Eaton Company had won the battle, but it lost the war. Seven years after opening its Government Street mall, the

PEMBROKE
DISCOVERY
CHATHAM S
HERALD ST.
FISGARD S
PANDORA A
JOHNSON S
YATES ST.
VIEW
FORT ST.
BROUGHTON
COURTNEY S
HUMBOLDT S
Fairmon
Empress
BELLEVILLE
SUPERIOR S
MICHIGAN S
TORONTO S
SIMCOE ST.

company declared bankruptcy. Soon the signs outside were changed to read "The Bay Centre," a reflection of its new ownership and a reminder that the complex stands opposite the site of the original Hudson's Bay Company fort.

⌘ Suspended from the ceiling in the Bay Centre is a large, four-sided clock. On two sides, clock faces display local "Victoria time" and the words "Victoria Eaton Centre Grand Opening 1990." On the other two sides, several smaller clock faces display the time in world cities and centres, above the strangely imperial-sounding slogan "Westward the course of Empire goes forth."

MUNRO'S BOOKS
1108 Government

Now it's a bookstore, but it used to be a bank—one of four that served the citizens of Victoria and the merchants along Government Street. However, this bank was different. Whereas the other three—Bank of British Columbia, Bank of Montreal and Union Bank of Canada—all occupied corner positions, the Royal Bank was in the middle of the block.

As if to compensate, its Thomas Hooper-designed granite facade and classical Tuscan columns gave it an air of permanence and stability. The banking hall was bathed in light filtered through a huge oval stained glass dome featuring the coats of arms of Canada's provinces, befitting an institution first established in 1864 as the Merchants Bank of Halifax.

After several decades the Royal Bank was modernized, and eventually, in the 1980s, it moved its operation one block east to Douglas Street. Bookseller Jim Munro bought the Government Street building in 1985 and restored it to its former glory. Months of painstakingly careful renovations revealed Hooper's original design elements, including marble floors and a cast-plaster ceiling. Above the pillared entrance, large letters spell out "Munro's Books of Victoria."

⌘ Next to Munro's Books, where book lovers browse in what was once a bank, Murchie's Tea & Coffee shop is run by descendants of Scottish-born tea blender John Murchie, who started in business in 1894.

⌘ **NEXT PAGE** Next to Murchie's, E.A. Morris's invites you to browse through an original, old-fashioned tobacco and cigar store. The adjacent five-storey structure, built in 1907 as a book and stationery store, is now home to the Bedford Regency Hotel.

QU
PR
PEMBROKE
DISCOVERY
CHATHAM
HERALD ST
FISGARD
PANDORA A
JOHNSON
YATES ST.
VIEW
FORT ST.
BROUGHTON
COURTNEY ST
HUMBOLDT S
Fairmo
Empre
BELLEVILL
ve
y
h
a
ERIOR ST.
HIGAN ST.
NTO ST.
Emily Carr
House

E.A. MORRIS TOBACCONIST
1116 Government

Step inside this fine example of an Edwardian smoke shop and take a step back in time to an era when cigar smoking was eminently acceptable, a popular pastime amongst the gentleman of the day.

Edward Morris opened this store well over a century ago. He was born in London, England, in 1858, the year gold was discovered on the Fraser River. At 19, he came through Victoria on his way to the British Columbia Interior, where he worked at several mines, but by the early 1890s he was ready to settle in Victoria for good. He bought a two-storey brick structure that had originally sold dry goods and set himself up as a tobacco merchant.

Before long, his store, which featured choice cigars and tobacco from England, was the largest of its kind on the west coast. By the time the Klondike gold rush was in full swing at the end of the 1890s, Old Morris Tobacconist was the largest distributor of smokers' supplies in the West.

In 1909, Morris decided to make major renovations at the store. Architect Thomas Hooper created an eye-catching storefront—the doorway, cut from Mexican onyx, was topped by a dome-shaped, leaded window—and completely redesigned the interior. Large wall mirrors reflected highly polished mahogany. Racks displayed pipes from all over the world. Classic carved columns marked the entrance to the humidor, a tile-lined, walk-in cabinet where cigars were stored.

When the store reopened, it featured a unique item specially ordered from San Francisco: an electrolier. This 2.5-metre-high column of Mexican onyx stood on a Nootka marble pedestal and was topped with a glass globe around an electric light bulb—one of the first such in Victoria. Cigar-level gas jets extended from either side. A cigar cutter and long cedar spills rested on the small shelf below. Morris's customers could use these to light up their cigars before leaving, which often encouraged new customers on the street outside to follow the enticing aroma back to the store.

Morris was still actively engaged in the business when he died at the relatively young age of 60, in 1937. Fortunately, subsequent owners have been keen to preserve the past. Thanks to them, the store's interior remains essentially the same. The sweet smell of pipe tobacco and the electrolier are still there too—reminders of the Government Street of days gone by, when people's "pipe dreams" paid for E.A. Morris's success.

SIDEWALK BRICKS
West side of Government
between Bastion and Broughton

Step carefully—there's history underfoot!

The bricks in the sidewalk on the west side of Government Street tell an interesting tale as they follow the eastern perimeter of old Fort Victoria.

Imagine six-metre-high cedar pickets along the line of these bricks. Trace the eight-sided shape of the fort's bastion on the corner of Government and Bastion Square. See the gap in the bricks just south of the intersection with Fort Street, where the back gate of the fort once stood. Observe the sharp corner that marks the southeast corner of the fort, in front of a retail store. And note that the bricks bear names, such as Harris, Albhouse, Hayward and Maynard.

Who were these people?

Every brick tells a story. Thomas Harris, for example, was elected first mayor of Victoria when the city was incorporated in 1862. Dora Albhouse, born here in 1898, taught elementary school for more than 40 years. Charles Hayward was an undertaker. Richard and Hannah Maynard took many of the interesting black-and-white photographs carefully preserved in British Columbia's provincial archives.

The bricks, placed here by the Greater Victoria Civic Archives Society, record the names of an interesting assortment of pioneers, entrepreneurs, artists, politicians and local businesses. They also record the names of First Nation chiefs who signed treaties with the HBC's James Douglas.

Amazingly, the bricks go unnoticed by all but the most discerning pedestrians, who appreciate that while life may be lived at eye

PEMBROKE S

DISCOVERY

CHATHAM S

HERALD ST.

FISGARD ST

PANDORA AV

JOHNSON S

YATES ST.

VIEW

FORT ST.

BROUGHTON

COURTNEY ST

HUMBOLDT S

Fairmont
Empress

BELLEVILLE S

SUPERIOR ST

MICHIGAN S

TORONTO ST

SIMCOE ST.

level, history is all around us. After all, these aren't just bricks; they're reminders of real people, pieces of history, the colour of courage, the shape of enterprise—a unique and fascinating peek into Victoria's past.

⌘ Bricks recording the names of early pioneers and businesses date from the 1970s, when Government Street's sidewalks were expanded to give walkers more room to wander. The bricks follow the eastern perimeter of Fort Victoria, from its southeast corner (outside Artina's jewellery store, near Broughton Street) to Bastion Square, where they mark the outline of the fort's eight-sided bastion, or gun tower, before continuing down into the square.

BASTION SQUARE
Government at Bastion Street

The busy, colourful Government Street entrance to Bastion Square belies its beginnings as a rough path along the northern perimeter of old Fort Victoria. Indeed, the landscape looked very different by the 1860s. Gone were the square, rather plain buildings of the fort. Gone were the gates through which so many hopefuls had headed toward a new life. Gone were the bastions that for two decades had guarded the Hudson's Bay Company's traders and labourers.

All that was left was Bastion Street, which started on Government where the north bastion had once stood and led west to what is now called Bastion Square, which was the site of the city's police barracks and jail. In the days of the gold rush, sentencing was swift and the penalty for crime was harsh. Close to a dozen murderers, miscreants and other miserable souls breathed their last on the jail yard's gallows. Rumour had it that some of those hanged were buried not in a cemetery but under the jail's exercise yard.

Victoria was a great, growing place where hotels, dance halls and saloons provided warmth and a welcome. One of the most popular watering holes, the Boomerang Saloon, was close to the jail. It was owned by British-born Ben Griffin, who had followed gold rushes all over the place—first to Australia, then San Francisco and now Victoria. Griffin gave his customers strong ale, good company and a generous offering of his self-penned poems. But it was his wife, Adelaide, who would be remembered long after Ben and the Boomerang were gone.

Without warning, the young and reasonably robust Adelaide died. She was buried, quickly but with due ceremony, in the Quadra Street Burying Ground. Ben was chief mourner. Surprisingly quickly, considering the shock of losing his wife, Ben bounced back, regaling his patrons with poetry and beer. As far as he was concerned, it was "business as usual." Or was it?

Adelaide might have been forgotten, at least by Ben, but it seemed she wasn't completely gone. One night not long after her burial, a group of merry miners weaving their unsteady way home from the Boomerang were shocked to see the ghostly form of a woman gliding across their path. Adelaide—for no one doubted it was her—was seen many more times near the Boomerang, and her death was never explained. If Ben, who died in 1881, held the answer to the mystery, he carried it to his grave.

PEMBROKE S
DISCOVERY
CHATHAM S
HERALD ST
FISGARD ST
PANDORA AV
JOHNSON S
YATES ST.
VIEW
FORT ST.
BROUGHTON
COURTNEY ST
HUMBOLDT S
Fairmont
Empress
BELLEVILLE S
SUPERIOR ST
MICHIGAN S
TORONTO ST
SIMCOE ST.

FORT VICTORIA
CIRCA
1858

⌘ OPPOSITE, TOP LEFT The entrance to Bastion Square, formerly Bastion Street, leads you past the former Bank of Montreal on one side (now the Irish Times Pub) and the Garrick's Head Pub on the other. OPPOSITE, TOP RIGHT An illustration of a bastion is featured on the Irish Times' side wall. Buildings that formerly housed law chambers are clustered in and around Bastion Square, conveniently close to architect Hermann Otto Tiedemann's provincial courthouse, which was completed in 1898. OPPOSITE, BOTTOM LEFT In the 1970s the courthouse became home to the Maritime Museum of BC. However, the third-floor courtroom, once presided over by Chief Justice Matthew Baillie Begbie (often referred to as "the hanging judge"), remains intact with its original judge's bench, jury benches and prisoner's dock. Court cases were heard here until 1962. It's said that Judge Begbie, who died in 1894, still haunts the building where he spent the last days of his working life. OPPOSITE, BOTTOM RIGHT The original top of the lighthouse on Trial Island, off the Oak Bay waterfront.

In the late 1880s, the city jail was demolished to make way for the brand-new provincial courthouse, which was soon joined by the Board of Trade Building, Burnes House Hotel, the law chambers and commercial ventures. Over the years, Bastion Street lost its splendour. Vehicles vied for a spot in what had become a huge public parking lot. Then, in 1965, the west end of the street was closed off to create Bastion Square, buildings were renovated and restored, and it became a people place once more.

The old courthouse, which for decades has been home to the Maritime Museum of BC, still holds pride of place in a square lined with offices, coffee shops, pubs and restaurants. Once, there was the clatter of hobnailed boots and the sound of hearty laughter as sailors, gold miners and townsfolk congregated here to have fun. Today, people still enjoy the ambience of Bastion Square. But late at night and in the early morning hours, only the ghosts remain.

IRISH TIMES PUB
1200 Government

The home of Thomas Harris, the man who became Victoria's first mayor, once stood on the northwest corner of Government Street and Bastion Square, where the Irish Times Pub now occupies the old Bank of Montreal.

Harris, an Englishman, came to Victoria in 1858 and set up the Liverpool Market at Government and Yates before opening a large butcher shop one block north. With the population of the little town increasing daily, the Queen's Meat Market was soon doing a roaring trade. Harris used the proceeds to build a fine home for his family at the corner of Bastion and Government. A large

PEMBROKE
DISCOVERY
CHATHAM S
HERALD ST.
FISGARD S
PANDORA A
JOHNSON S
YATES ST.
VIEW
FORT ST.
BROUGHTON
COURTNEY S
HUMBOLDT S
Fairmon
Empress
BELLEVILLE S
SUPERIOR S
MICHIGAN S
TORONTO ST
SIMCOE ST.

brick edifice, splendid for its time, it stood out among the simpler buildings surrounding it.

Harris described himself as "just an 'umble tradesman," but humble he certainly was not. Nor was he ever short of an opinion or likely to back down from an argument. Bald of head and florid of face, he was a veritable giant of a man with an ego to match. What he lacked in formal education, he made up for in firmness and sheer physical presence.

In early 1862, after dabbling in everything from business ventures to real estate to shipping, Harris, now 46, was ready to try politics. By August he had thrown his hat into the ring for mayor. In just two years, Victoria had produced a bridge across James Bay, purpose-built government offices, hotels, a jail, a firehall, five churches, a theatre, schools and a hospital. It was an exciting place to live—and to lead. Harris campaigned carefully, and when Governor Douglas signed a bill passed by the legislative assembly that declared Victoria a city, he was ready.

As elections go, this one was nothing if not straightforward. About 600 people gathered at the hustings. There was no secret ballot, and Harris had only one opponent. Voting was by show of hands—a few for Alfred Waddington, a veritable forest for Harris.

Amid wild excitement and cheering, Harris became the first mayor of Victoria.

In August 1862, Victoria city council met for the first time in the police barracks alongside the county jail. However, it was the second meeting that cemented Harris's reputation for weighty discourse. One minute, he was looking over the judge's bench; the next, he had disappeared behind it. His armchair had collapsed beneath his considerable weight, and he had been unceremoniously dumped onto the floor—alighting, according to His Worship, on that portion of the breeches which wears out first.

Quickly composing themselves, council members turned their attention to more serious matters, striking a Committee of Nuisances to deal with troublesome problems of the day. Soon the word was out: straying pigs and goats would be impounded; the firing of guns and pistols in the city would not be tolerated; and horse-drawn traffic was to keep to the left-hand side of the road, with a travelling speed not exceeding eight miles per hour. The first city council, with Harris at its head, was off to a flying start.

Harris worked hard and played hard. Known for his love of good food, good wine and horse racing, he was never happier than

⌘ TOP The Irish Times pub on the north corner of Bastion Square is housed in the old Bank of Montreal building, built in 1897 on the site of first mayor Thomas Harris's home.

⌘ RIGHT In the summer, visitors to Bastion Square enjoy open-air restaurants and artisans' markets.

PEMBROKE
DISCOVERY
CHATHAM S
HERALD ST
FISGARD S
PANDORA A
JOHNSON
YATES ST.
VIEW
FORT ST.
BROUGHTON
COURTNEY S
HUMBOLDT
Fairmor
Empres
BELLEVILLE
ERIOR S
HIGAN
ONTO S
COE ST.

when thundering around Beacon Hill Park's racetrack on his favourite mount, George. He was a competent jockey and won almost every race he entered.

Unfortunately, he didn't fare as well in the council chamber. In 1863 he defeated his opponent by a much narrower margin, and a year later decided to retire from civic politics. All was not well on the financial front either. Having spent money faster than he could make it, Harris leased the lower floor of his Government Street residence to a bank and moved his family to another home.

Then came another blow. While driving out on the West Saanich Road, he fell from his buggy, sustaining fractures to an arm and a leg. He never did regain full use of his limbs. Nevertheless, he continued to be politically active and was high sheriff of Victoria when he died, at the age of 68, in 1884. Bishop Cridge officiated at the funeral service at the Reformed Episcopal Church. Then Victoria's first, feisty, Falstaffian mayor was finally laid to rest.

TROUNCE ALLEY
1200-block Government

Across Government Street from the old Bank of Montreal, you might look at the street sign saying "Trounce Alley" and wonder: Why does it have such a strange name? Who was trounced here? When did it happen? And why?

Fear not. Although the dictionary tells us that *trounce* means "beat severely, or thrash," the only person who ever took a trouncing in connection with this alley was the one who created it—a fellow named Thomas Trounce.

Trounce was another early European arrival who left his mark on our city's streets. Born in Cornwall, England, in 1813, Trounce and his wife, Jane, set forth in the 1840s, sailing first to Van Diemen's Land (now Tasmania), then to California. In 1858 they sailed to Victoria on a steamer stuffed with gold seekers.

They found a small Hudson's Bay Company settlement blinking its eyes in disbelief. All had been peaceful here until news of Fraser River riches spread south, and thousands of eager prospectors came to buy licences to dig for gold. Now it was pandemonium, and there was nowhere for people to stay. At first the Trounces slept in the "tent town" just north of the fort; then they moved to a frame cottage nearby. Trounce quickly established himself as an architect and contractor, and before long he was able to build a more salubrious dwelling near the colonial administration offices in James Bay.

Now he could concentrate on developing his business. He bought prime land at the south end of the block between Broad and Government Streets, rubbing his hands with glee in anticipation of collecting rent from store owners on all sides. Then came a nasty shock. He had been told that View Street was to be extended to Wharf Street. It made sense—after all, what is a View Street without a view? However, a sudden and unexpected property deal saw a large chunk of land sold to businessman J. J. Southgate, who promptly fenced it off, causing View Street to come to an abrupt halt at Broad.

Trounce solved the problem in 1859 by cutting a lane through the middle of his property from Broad Street to Government. Trounce Alley was born, with stores fronting onto the alley. Eventually, after a major fire in the area in 1910, city council decided to extend View Street through to Government after all, affording Trounce's tenants entry from not one but two sides.

Trounce was a member of city council and the architect responsible for several commercial downtown structures, including the Green Building on Broad Street, and John Weiler's furniture factory (now the Counting House) at Broughton and Broad. He was also

⌘ Iron gates at both ends of Thomas Trounce's alley guaranteed privacy at the close of each working day. Until 1900 they were closed for a token one day a year to retain ownership of the thoroughfare, but since then have never been closed.

PEMBROKE
DISCOVERY
CHATHAM
HERALD ST
FISGARD S
PANDORA A
JOHNSON
YATES ST
VIEW
FORT ST.
BROUGHTON
COURTNEY S
HUMBOLDT
Fairmor
Empres
BELLEVILLE
SUPERIOR S
MICHIGAN
TORONTO S
SIMCOE ST.

an upstanding pillar of the community—he became Grand Master of the Masonic Temple at Fisgard and Douglas—and a solid supporter of the Methodist (now United) Church close to his James Bay home.

Trounce died there in 1900, aged 87. The house is long gone, its place taken by an apartment building. In 1896 the Bank of Montreal was built on the corner of Bastion and Government Streets, so View Street still doesn't have a view. But Trounce Alley is there to this day—a reminder of the man who refused to let a blocked road take the edge off his business success.

W. & J. WILSON CLOTHIERS
1221 Government

On the corner of Government Street and Thomas Trounce's alley, British-born brothers William and Joseph Wilson opened their clothing store in 1862. It might have been just another one in a row, but thanks to Thomas Trounce cutting an alleyway through his property in 1859, the Wilsons' store ended up on a corner, with double the space for display windows to entice passersby.

Born in London, England, in 1838, William Wilson was 24 years old when he learned there was gold in the Cariboo and sailed around Cape Horn to find it. When his ship anchored in 1862, Wilson found the small, newly incorporated city of Victoria brimming with business opportunities. The Cariboo turned out to be a lot farther away than he had supposed. It would cost a lot of money to transport the goods he had brought with him. Why not sell them in Victoria and invest the proceeds in a local venture?

He bought the stock of a firm that had gone bankrupt and opened his own store on the premises. It was just a simple log building on the east side of Government Street, but business was so brisk that the next spring he decided to follow his original plan and check out the Cariboo. He left the Victoria store in the capable hands of his brother Joseph, newly arrived from England via Panama.

William summered in Barkerville and wintered in Victoria. Four years later, with the men's clothing store in the Cariboo a success and the mines worked out, he returned to Victoria for good. Joseph, meanwhile, had not been idle. Patriarch Joseph Wilson Sr., still in England, had ensured a steady supply of merchandise, and profits continued to climb.

William had precious little time for romance. But one day in 1864 he met a young

⌘ Enlarged and remodelled many times, W. & J. Wilson Clothiers is the oldest surviving Government Street store operating under the original name, having conducted business here since 1862. In 1963, picturesque street lamps were mounted in Trounce Alley to commemorate W. & J. Wilson's 100th anniversary.

lady named Elizabeth Eilbeck who was visiting her sister and brother-in-law in Victoria. They married on New Year's Day, 1865. The union lasted 40 years and produced six children.

Meanwhile, W. & J. Wilson's became a much-respected business in Victoria. The Government Street location secured steady traffic with every biweekly mail boat. A reputation for quality fabrics and finely tailored garments from the old country attracted a faithful following and guaranteed growth. The log building on Government Street was demolished in favour of more modern premises, and eventually W. & J. Wilson's spread its wings and opened stores in several other cities in Western Canada.

William maintained a high profile in the community by serving for many years as a member of the school board and, from 1878 to 1882, as a member of the legislative assembly. Joseph, who never married, died in 1900. By then his nephew, William's son Joseph, who had joined the business some 16 years earlier, was managing the store. The company's premises were enlarged in 1905 and again in 1912 to supply the demand for quality clothing.

William Wilson's home in Rockland was a very social place—five sons and a daughter saw to that. Life was not without sadness, however. Before the turn of the century, Elizabeth died at the age of 60.

PEMBROKE

DISCOVERY

CHATHAM S

HERALD ST.

FISGARD S

PANDORA A

JOHNSON S

YATES ST.

VIEW

FORT ST.

BROUGHTON

COURTNEY S

HUMBOLDT

Fairmon
Empres

BELLEVILLE

SUPERIOR S

MICHIGAN

TORONTO S

William moved in with his daughter, who lived in James Bay, and died there in 1922, at the age of 84. A testament to their tenacity, the store survives right where the Wilson brothers built it all those decades ago.

YATES STREET

When you stand on Government and look up or down Yates Street, you'll notice that it's quite a bit wider than the streets that run parallel—a fitting reminder of the enterprising man who gave his name to this thoroughfare in the days when the Hudson's Bay Company reigned supreme.

Scottish-born James Yates was a shipwright and carpenter who signed on with the company in 1848. He and Mary, his bride of two short weeks, set sail a year later, bound for the HBC outpost on the southern tip of Vancouver Island. They were an interesting pair. James was a big man and, on occasion, fierce of temper; Mary, by contrast, was small, gentle and soothing—traits that would serve her well in the months and years to come.

In May 1849, after a wild, midwinter voyage around Cape Horn, the *Harpooner*'s passengers were much relieved to reach their destination—until they realized that their new surroundings hardly matched the Company's glowing description of its Pacific Northwest headquarters. For one thing, accommodations at the fort might have been adequate for rough-and-ready fur traders, but they were barely suitable for people accustomed to more comfortable surroundings.

James Douglas promised to pass on the newcomers' complaints, but as far as Yates was concerned, it was way too late. Finding Douglas impossible to deal with, he left to seek his fortune in California. When he returned later that year to fetch his wife and family, he was thrown into the fort's bastion as penance for reneging on his contract. Released after a month, he flatly refused to work for Douglas again and was allowed to assume independent status.

His new business was as far removed from carpentering as could be and a great deal more lucrative. Yates became a wine and spirit merchant, and proud owner of the settlement's first watering hole—the Ship Inn, down on the waterfront. This did nothing to endear him to Douglas, but enabled him to buy several town lots from the HBC. When prospectors en route to the Fraser River swarmed into the settlement in the summer of 1858, Yates leased the land he had bought east of his tavern to merchants, saloon keepers and others who threw up wooden shanties to serve the gold-hungry hordes. Soon, handsome brick-and-stone buildings on the street that took his name were bringing in an equally handsome income for their owner. By 1860, James Yates was arguably the richest man in town.

Four years later, the fort where the Yates family had spent their earliest days in Victoria was just a memory. The HBC outpost had become a city. Unfortunately, Yates Street, far from being the grand central thoroughfare that its owner had envisaged, was now an area filled with bawdy houses, brothels and belligerent drunks. Victoria was in a state of decline. It was time to move on. Yates took his family back to Scotland. His sons returned to Victoria some years later, and their descendants know all about the extra-wide street that still bears their ancestor's name.

Even though his street has been revitalized with the careful and imaginative creation of commercial, condominium and live-work spaces behind original facades, James Yates wouldn't recognize it today. Only the Yates

⌘ Lower Yates Street, with its wholesale outlets and numerous saloons, hotels, restaurants and offices, was the very heart of the commercial district in early-20th-century Victoria. Over a century later, many of the original buildings on the south side of the street are long gone, but the north side remains virtually intact, reminding us that commercial enterprises once shared the street with the former Majestic Theatre (1861) and the Oriental Hotel (1883), now revitalized as a condominium development (centre). Farther down the street, provision merchant Thomas Earle's 1900 premises have been joined to wholesale grocer Simon Leiser's 1896 warehouse, which contained the first commercial elevator in downtown Victoria. Wood-blocked Waddington Alley runs along the west side of Leiser's building, connecting Yates and Johnson Streets. On the south side of Yates, Commercial Alley connects it with Bastion Square.

PEMBROKE
DISCOVERY
CHATHAM S
HERALD ST.
FISGARD S
PANDORA A
JOHNSON S
YATES ST.
VIEW
FORT ST.
BROUGHTON
COURTNEY S
HUMBOLDT S
Fairmon
Empress
BELLEVILLE
SUPERIOR S
MICHIGAN
TORONTO S
SIMCOE ST.

⌘ In 1899 the horse-and-buggy era neared its end with the introduction of newfangled streetcars adorned with lights, bells, hand-painted route signs and advertisements. The streetcar in this photo followed a route from Hillside via Yates and Government, across the James Bay Bridge, and along Birdcage Walk and Superior Street to the Outer Wharf, just north of Ogden Point. After a snowfall, the tracks disappeared under snow that residents and businesspeople had shovelled off their roofs and sidewalks. This car is shown just before turning the corner from Yates onto Government, in the days when Government was still a two-way street. At left, a uniformed policeman keeps a watchful eye on wandering pedestrians, who were allowed to stop and board the car at any point along the route. The last Victoria streetcar ran on July 5, 1948. It was a black-letter day for Victorians, who were also losing their wood-blocked streets, an innovative idea that spread through the downtown core after Alfred Waddington "paved" his alley with wooden blocks to cut down on the clatter of horse-and-cart traffic during the gold-rush days.

PEMBROKE

DISCOVERY

CHATHAM S

HERALD ST.

FISGARD S

PANDORA A

JOHNSON S

YATES ST.

VIEW

FORT ST.

BROUGHTON

COURTNEY S

HUMBOLDT S

Fairmon
Empres

BELLEVILLE

SUPERIOR S

MICHIGAN

TORONTO S

SIMCOE ST.

Block (1244–1252 Wharf Street), site of the old Ship Inn, and 1218 Wharf Street, which face us in the distance at the foot of Yates Street, hint at the Victoria he and his sons once knew.

JOHNSON STREET
AND MARKET SQUARE

A glance down Lower Johnson Street today reveals a road lined with offices, boutiques and specialty stores, but yesterday . . . Johnson Street simply didn't exist. In Victoria's earliest days, the settlement was bordered by Wharf, Government and Yates Streets. North of Yates, a ravine provided a conduit for waters flowing westward to empty into the harbour.

When men first flooded Victoria en route to the goldfields in 1858, the Chinese among them settled on the north side of the ravine, which could only be crossed at this point by a wooden footbridge. On the ravine's south side, wood frame stores, saloons and hotels competed with each other to satisfy the newcomers' needs. During the cold winter months, gold miners returned to Victoria with gold dust to spare and nothing to use it for but their own enjoyment. In those rough-and-ready times, drinking, dancing, gambling and fighting were the order of the day. Aboriginals and whites caroused together, while the Chinese—teased and ridiculed by people who neither understood them nor took an interest in their culture—kept mostly to themselves on the far side of the ravine, creating Canada's first Chinatown.

Fast-forward a few decades, and everything had changed. By the late 1890s the wooden shacks and shanties were gone. The ravine had been filled in to create Johnson Street, and its brick stores, saloons and handsome hotels catered to a whole new generation of gold seekers—men who came to mine the Klondike.

Businesses edged the block bordered by Johnson, Store, Pandora and Government Streets. At its centre, a courtyard shared by the buildings on all four sides formed a sort of no man's land where two cultures—one white, the other Chinese—carried on a mutually beneficial but often uneasy coexistence.

Johnson Street divided a town whose north and south sections, although geographically close, were worlds apart. South of Johnson, most of Victoria's citizens conducted their lives with genteel respectability. Businesses along Government Street catered to the wealthy. Wharf Street merchants imported goods from all over the world. A new legislature graced the south side of the Inner Harbour. There was talk

of cleaning up the foul-smelling James Bay mud flats and maybe even building a major new hotel.

The north side of town was another story. The Cariboo gold rush had been followed by a two-decade downturn in fortunes, and recovery had been slow. But a resurgence of ocean-going trade created a demand for ship supplies and repair, providing business for chandlers and metalworkers. The Esquimalt & Nanaimo Railway connected Victoria with Nanaimo. Opium factories in Chinatown brought in a lucrative income for its 4,000-plus residents.

Merchants plied their wares, dance halls and saloons enticed, bawdy houses bustled. In the 1890s, it was said of Johnson Street

⌘ Lower Johnson Street—known as LoJo—is a mecca for shoppers who enjoy the brightly painted historic facades and appreciate the latest fashions in clothing and shoes. Between Johnson and Pandora Streets, buried in the heart of Victoria's Old Town, Market Square forms a fascinating link with the not-so-distant past. Iron gates provide access from Johnson Street. Staircases lead down to the lower level of the square, which is directly above the deepest part of the old Johnson Street ravine. A breezeway on the square's north side connects it with Pandora Avenue.

that if a man was drunk, he could roll out of one bar and fall right into another. Sealing fleets brought business. The Klondike beckoned. Sailors and prospectors flooded into town, and Johnson Street came alive again.

The Bossi brothers, originally from Italy, invested their grocery sales profits into real estate, erecting commercial buildings on Johnson, Store and Pandora. Others followed suit. Hotels had names like Grand Pacific, Strand, Senator, Station and Empire. Success was in the air . . . until the First World War brought everything to a grinding halt.

The effects of the resulting economic downturn lingered for decades, and by the late 1960s, Old Town and Chinatown showed signs of deep decay. In an effort to revitalize this once-prosperous area, the city embarked on a frenzy of new development. Concerned citizens formed a heritage preservation society to identify and protect historic structures. Mayor Peter Pollen spearheaded a move to rehabilitate Old Town. Local businessman Sam Bawlf and his brother Nicholas, a restoration architect, were major players, preserving heritage buildings and creating the multi-level retail mall we now call Market Square.

One hundred years ago, this area's reputation left a lot to be desired. Today, Lower Johnson Street, with its mix of businesses, apartments and brightly painted facades, features the latest fashions in clothing and shoes. Market Square houses shops and eateries, hosts outdoor festivals and is home to the winter market. And on the wall in the breezeway connecting the square with Pandora Avenue, a display of archival photos describes the square's historical connection to the Chinatown of days gone by.

SITE OF LAWRENCE GOODACRE'S STORE
1300-block Government at Johnson

Hard to imagine, isn't it, that once Johnson Street was the northern border of town. In those days, Government Street ended here. Fortunately for Lawrence Goodacre, by the 1870s the ravine had been filled in and his business was more than holding its own.

Goodacre had arrived here from England in the mid-1860s, at the age of 18. Victoria was a growing city and soon to become the capital of British Columbia—a splendid spot for an ambitious young fellow with a solid background in butchering. He went into partnership with John Stafford, who had recently taken over the Queen's Meat Market, a Government Street

⌘ The former Romano Theatre (now Christmas Village) at the corner of Government and Johnson—once the site of Lawrence Goodacre's butcher shop—was owned by the Quagliotti brothers, who also owned the nearby Grand Theatre (later Empress, then Rio) in the days when movie theatres were all the rage.

business started by Thomas Harris, our city's first mayor.

Stafford became ill in 1876, then died. Left to pick up the pieces, Goodacre looked after the store—and Stafford's grieving widow and children. The two men had been close friends, so no one was surprised when Maria Stafford and Lawrence Goodacre became man and wife.

Goodacre took on John Dooley as a partner, and before long they were the top money-producer in their class, serving Her Majesty's Royal Navy, the Dominion government and several large corporations, not to mention local hotels, restaurants and households.

As the years went by, Goodacre recruited his sons into the business and became more and more involved with politics. Elected alderman for Johnson Street ward in 1889, he served on and off until 1906. Goodacre worked at his store and involved himself in civic and social affairs until he was 80 years old. Then he retired. Two years later he was gone, a victim of heart disease.

There's little on Government Street today to remind us of Goodacre's presence in our town. However, in recognition of his service to the Parks Board—and the fact that his store provided meat for the animals in the Beacon Hill Park zoo—the park's largest body of water, Goodacre Lake, was named in his honour.

NEW ENGLAND HOTEL
1312 Government

Many Victoria residents and visitors have "sweet memories" of an ice-cream shop that for many years operated in the lovely old

PEMBROKE

DISCOVERY

CHATHAM

HERALD ST

FISGARD S

PANDORA

JOHNSON

YATES ST

VIEW

FORT ST.

BROUGHTON

COURTNEY S

HUMBOLDT

Fairmor
Empres

BELLEVILLE

SUPERIOR S

MICHIGAN

TORONTO S

SIMCOE ST.

LIGHTING THE WAY The turn-of-the-century-style streetlights along our main downtown thoroughfares remind us of the Government Street of days gone by. It was Alfred Morley, a far-seeing fellow who served three separate terms as Victoria's mayor during the first two decades of the 1900s, who lobbied to have cluster lights installed downtown. The city, he pointed out, was not just a commercial centre; it was fast becoming a popular place to visit. Victoria needed something different, and distinctive streetlights, he decided, would do the trick. They called them "Morley's Follies," but in 1910 they installed the globe-shaped lights anyway, mostly to humour the mayor.

Long after Morley was gone, the streetlights remained. In 2010, 20 new lamp standards were installed along Government Street between Belleville and Yates. Each one features an ornamental turn-of-the-century-style lamp at the top, with the familiar globe shapes nestling underneath and, in spring and summer, flower baskets dangling below. If Alfred Morley were here today, he'd be thrilled to see that cluster lights still line our downtown streets, just as he intended they should over 100 years ago.

building halfway along this block on the west side of Government. There's an unhappy connection between this building and the Rogers' Chocolates shop farther down the street, which we'll talk more about in a moment.

In the meantime, look up and you'll see that the building's fourth-floor facade boasts the words "Established 1858." That's when—at the very beginning of the Fraser River gold rush—George and Fritz Steitz founded an eatery on this site. Their New England Restaurant quickly earned a favourable reputation up and down the coast.

By 1864 the Steitz brothers were itching to get to the goldfields, and the restaurant was sold. In 1877 new owners Michael Young and his son Louis opened a bakery and added a room "For Ladies and Families Exclusively," which served reasonably priced meals at all hours. Soon they were ready to expand. The old 1858 structure was demolished. Architect John Teague was hired to design its replacement, and in October 1892 the four-storey New England Hotel celebrated its grand opening.

Teague's unusually tall, cast-iron bay windows made for an impressive sight. High ceilings complemented full-length windows

hung with plush velvet drapes. The main floor housed a huge dining room and salons for private parties. Extensive wine cellars and the bakery's great stone ovens were in the basement.

In the early 1900s the hotel was at the height of its glory. Guests were appreciative, food was cheap and business was brisker than it had ever been, even when the hotel was the scene of a tragedy. In 1905, 15-year-old Fred Rogers, reluctant heir to his parents' chocolate-making empire down the street, shot himself to death with a handgun in one of the hotel's rooms. (For the story of the Rogers family, see page 74.)

Fortunes changed over the years as the First World War, a Depression and the Second World War took their toll. One after another, owners struggled to make the hotel pay by renting rooms, running restaurants and leasing space to a variety of enterprises, including a tattoo parlour, an antique shop and a dance hall. By 1982 the building needed major upgrades, and the upper-floor renters had been forced to leave. Its owner opened an ice-cream parlour at street level but left the upper floors alone.

Today, the New England Hotel has been given a new lease on life. A local developer

PEMBROKE

DISCOVERY

CHATHAM S

HERALD ST.

FISGARD S

PANDORA A

JOHNSON S

YATES ST.

VIEW

FORT ST.

BROUGHTON

COURTNEY S

HUMBOLDT S

Fairmon
Empress

BELLEVILLE

SUPERIOR S

MICHIGAN

TORONTO S

SIMCOE ST.

has restored and preserved properties along and around Government Street, including the lovely old building that once housed a vibrant business, launched on this site over a century and a half ago.

PRIOR BUILDING
1401 Government / 601–614 Johnson

On the northeast corner of Government and Johnson Streets, a plain building devoid of ornament or character belies the business that once flourished there under the ownership of hardware merchant and long-ago premier Edward Gawler Prior.

The Yorkshire-born Prior arrived in Victoria at the age of 20, in 1873. Seven years later he went into business with Alfred Fellows. By 1891 he had incorporated the firm as E.G. Prior & Company Ltd., with just under 100 employees in Victoria, branch operations in Vancouver and Kamloops, and offices in London and New York. As well as hardware items, his three-storey building housed carriages, wagons and all kinds of

⌘ The New England Hotel's tall, narrow, unusually shaped windows made it stand out from other buildings along Government Street, just as it does today.

⌘ E.G. Prior's hardware emporium was a force to be reckoned with in early Victoria. Once characterized by huge arched entranceways and windows and plenty of curb space for delivery carts, it still commands the corner where Prior built it, well over a century ago.

farm machinery, while a warehouse a few blocks north on Government Street provided storage for goods imported from all over the world.

Prior became British Columbia's 11th premier in 1902, and in 1919 was appointed lieutenant-governor of the province. He had reached the peak of his political ambitions, but less than a year after his appointment, he

was taken ill and died at the age of 67. His premises survive to this day, but E.G. Prior would be hard put to recognize his building—or indeed the city where he made his mark all those years ago.

DE COSMOS BUILDING
1400-block Government

This block-long building on the west side of Government reminds us of a major player in Victoria's early days, a fellow with an improbable name—Amor De Cosmos.

De Cosmos was born plain William Alexander Smith in Nova Scotia in 1825. A good education gave him confidence beyond his years, and skills developed at the Dalhousie Debating Club involved him in word battles that helped relieve the boredom of his life as a grocery clerk. By 1851 he couldn't stand it any longer. He was 26, young and ambitious, and on the other side of the continent, people were digging for gold. He travelled to California, and by the summer of 1853 was working as a photographer, creating pictorial records of miners and their properties.

Among his fellow gold seekers, there were several Smiths, some William Smiths,

PEMBROKE S
DISCOVERY S
CHATHAM ST
HERALD ST
FISGARD ST
PANDORA AV
JOHNSON S
YATES ST.
VIEW S
FORT ST.
BROUGHTON
COURTNEY ST
HUMBOLDT S
Fairmont
Empress
BELLEVILLE S
SUPERIOR ST
MICHIGAN S
TORONTO ST.
SIMCOE ST.

even another William Alexander Smith. It was confusing to say the least, and downright irritating when post office mail went astray. Deciding to change his name to one with more flair, one that would make him stand out from the crowd, Bill Smith chose a moniker with elements of three foreign languages—*Amor* from the Latin, *De* from the French and *Cosmos* from the Greek. Perfect for a man with far-ranging interests and lofty ideals. By the end of February 1854, it was official. Goodbye Bill Smith, hello Amor De (capital-D) Cosmos, "Lover of the Universe."

Prospering under his new identity, De Cosmos ventured into mining, trading and land speculation, and in 1858 journeyed to Victoria. There he discovered that the fellow in charge of Fort Victoria, Vancouver Island and the mainland colony wielded incredible power. James Douglas, it appeared, hired his own relatives for key positions regardless of their qualifications, and he favoured the company that had hired him, decades earlier, over the country that had appointed him governor of the colony.

Sensing a challenge, and seeing an opportunity to make his mark, De Cosmos launched his most ambitious enterprise to date—a newspaper called the *British Colonist*. The first issue, which hit the streets of Victoria on December 11, 1858, signalled the start of a personal and public crusade that would continue for decades to come.

De Cosmos was a thorn in Governor Douglas's side until the latter's dying day. But he was also a tireless champion of the province he now called home. Elected to the legislature in 1863, he strongly supported Victoria's right to be called the capital of British Columbia and was among the first to push for British Columbia's entry into Confederation. In 1872 he was appointed premier and president of the executive council and represented Victoria in the House of Commons.

Ten years later, De Cosmos retired and gradually started to fail. Once impeccable in frock coat and silk hat, he now looked haggard and gaunt and was prone to such frequent outbursts that people avoided him on the street. Eventually he was declared mentally unfit. When he died in July 1897, few Victorians attended his funeral—an ignominious end for a man who, despite his penchant for pouting, ranting and long-winded speeches, had achieved much for the province of British Columbia.

PEMBROKE S
DISCOVERY S
CHATHAM ST
HERALD ST.
FISGARD ST
PANDORA AV
JOHNSON ST
YATES ST.
VIEW S
FORT ST.
BROUGHTON S
COURTNEY ST
HUMBOLDT ST
Fairmont
Empress
BELLEVILLE S
SUPERIOR ST.
MICHIGAN ST
TORONTO ST.
SIMCOE ST.

The 1885 De Cosmos block has been sold and altered many times over the years. De Cosmos's original building stood at the block's north end. At its south end, the Wilson–Dalby Block, added in 1896, once housed a prestigious hotel. Today's bland, featureless structure, bereft of its original decorative elements, does little to remind us of the flamboyant fellow who built it in 1885—Amor De Cosmos, newspaper editor, politician and self-proclaimed "lover of the universe."

⌘ At the end of the 1890s, the Victoria Hotel, at the south end of the De Cosmos block, was considered one of the city's finest. Its 70-plus steam-heated rooms featured baths, bells and other newfangled contraptions—all for $2 per day. The block's grand corner roof decoration and arched upper windows have disappeared. Today's utilitarian look hides the story of the man whose name still intrigues—Amor De Cosmos.

CHINATOWN

It seems fitting that the intersection of Government with Pandora is especially wide. The area ahead of you, bounded by Government, Store, Pandora and Herald Streets, tells its own special story from Victoria's past. Welcome to Canada's earliest Chinatown!

Like so many others in the late 1850s, Chinese men were first drawn here by the glitter of Fraser River gold. When the gold ran out, many took their hard-earned money back to China, but some chose to stay in Victoria. Their wooden shacks were clustered along the north side of the Johnson Street ravine. Land was cheaper there, and living in close proximity allowed the mostly male population to preserve and protect its culture and traditions.

By 1861, Chinese people owned and lived in the area now bounded by Douglas, Fisgard, Store and Pandora, as well as some lots to the north and south and along the nearby waterfront. Most of their commercial activities—stores and other businesses—could be found on what was then called Cormorant Street, where Centennial Square and Lower Pandora Avenue are today.

The white population called this area "Chinatown" and viewed the newcomers with

⌘ Ping Tsing's Red Dragon sculpture, lurking at the north end of the De Cosmos block near the corner of Pandora Avenue, marks the beginning of Victoria's Chinatown. The cast-iron panels on the fence outside 599 Pandora were rescued during demolition of the Driard Hotel (now part of the Bay Centre).

suspicion and concern. They were happy enough to have them as houseboys or to buy the fresh vegetables Chinese gardeners brought to the back doors of their homes, but they didn't understand the Chinese or their culture, and they certainly didn't see—or treat—the Chinese as equals.

In the mid-1880s, when the cross-Canada railroad reached the West Coast, Victoria's Chinese population exploded. Thousands of men had been brought from China to perform the dangerous, back-breaking work of building the railroad. Those who survived (many did not) found themselves at the end of the line without enough money to return to China. Rather than stay in the raw, rough city called Vancouver, many chose to join Victoria's established Chinese community. Others followed. During the last decade of the 19th century and the first decade of the 20th, Victoria's six-block Chinatown was home to more than 95 percent of Canada's total Chinese population.

Feeling threatened, the white community tried to stem the flow of immigrants by imposing a head tax on all Chinese entering Canada. But some people wanted Chinese immigration to continue. The Chinese were hard workers, deferential and uncomplaining, willing to perform menial tasks—labouring, market gardening, laundering and domestic work—that white men refused to do. And so the two groups forged a somewhat uneasy coexistence.

The Chinese continued to work hard in their market gardens and as servants in people's homes while carefully preserving their own centuries-old traditions. In Chinatown, large and successful import businesses lined the perimeters, presenting a bland, businesslike face to the world. Behind their facades, crowded buildings housed a

thriving community, while an intricate network of alleyways guarded the entrances to the places where men followed traditional leisure-time pursuits. Chinatown's physical and societal separation made it seem even more exotic to the white citizens of Victoria, whose ignorance and suspicion of Chinese customs continued. At the same time, some whites were drawn to the intriguing areas of "the forbidden city," particularly its brothels, gambling dens and opium houses.

Despite ongoing discrimination, which continued well into the 20th century (Chinese Canadians were not given full rights of citizenship until 1967), the residents of Chinatown maintained their traditional way of life. Over the decades, although many residents gradually moved to other parts of

PEMBROKE S
DISCOVERY
CHATHAM S
HERALD ST.
FISGARD ST
PANDORA A\
JOHNSON S
YATES ST.
VIEW
FORT ST.
BROUGHTON
COURTNEY ST
HUMBOLDT S
Fairmon
Empress
BELLEVILLE S
SUPERIOR ST
MICHIGAN S
TORONTO ST
SIMCOE ST.

the city, the original structures and much of the essence of Chinatown have remained.

Today, a stroll down Lower Pandora Avenue, through Fan Tan Alley, along Fisgard Street and through Dragon Alley to Herald Street will take you past a fascinating mix of commercial and administrative buildings, tongs (meeting halls), temples, fruit and vegetable vendors, curio shops, Asian ware stores and galleries, herb stores and more.

On Fisgard Street, which is packed with restaurants, stores selling local and exotic produce, and galleries displaying unique pieces, look down—Chinese characters are marked out in bricks on certain stretches of sidewalk. Look at the walls—colourful murals display the countenances and costumes of those who once lived here. And at Fisgard and Government, look up. The carefully designed and intricately decorated Gate of Harmonious Interest is a permanent reminder that, thanks to the courage and tenacity of those early Chinese arrivals, the once "forbidden" city remains a vital part of Victoria—the cultural anchor at the north end of Government Street's "heritage mile."

FAN TAN ALLEY
Between Pandora and Fisgard

Some say it is the narrowest street in North America, but for the people who lived there in the latter part of the 1800s, it was the main access to the area they called home. Fan Tan Alley was once the main route to Victoria's Chinatown.

In those days, almost all of Chinatown's inhabitants were men, who worked long and hard for very little. Far from their homes and families, they amused themselves with typical Chinese pursuits, including the theatre, celebration of traditional festivals, visits to the temple or the brothel, and indoor games such

⌘ OPPOSITE TOP Looking down the north side of Pandora (formerly Cormorant) Avenue toward the harbour. The 1894 Loo Chew Fan Building, headquarters of the Hoy Sun Ning Yang Benevolent Association since 1904, marks the entrance to Fan Tan Alley.

⌘ OPPOSITE BOTTOM Looking down Lower Fisgard toward Wharf Street, from where the Gate of Harmonious Interest stands today, we see the spire of the Chinese Methodist Church (demolished in 1962) on the right. On the left, Chung Lung & Co. was one of four stores on the main floor of the Loo Tai Cho building. Just beyond it is the Fisgard Street entrance to Fan Tan Alley and the building that houses the Chinese-Canadian Cultural Association.

Chinatown and Chinese Church, Victoria, B.C.

106.914

⌘ OPPOSITE The focal point of Chinatown, the Gate of Harmonious Interest was erected in 1981. Its Chinese name—Tong Ji Men—means "to work together with one heart" (Tongxin Xieli) and "to help each other to achieve harmony" (Hezhong Gongji). The 11.5-metre gate's design follows the principle of symmetry, and the art on the gate illustrates the Chinese concept of the Yin-Yang equilibrium in nature. The stone lions in front of the gate were donated by Suzhou, Victoria's sister city in China. The gate itself is a permanent monument to the Chinese heritage in the city and a unique way of preserving Chinatown's historic past.

as chess, chuck-luck and fan-tan—a Chinese game of chance.

Played in China for centuries, fan-tan was a simple game that required only an ordinary table and a collection of small objects—usually buttons, beads or coins. The banker covered the objects with a metal bowl, and the players around the table placed bets on the number of objects that might be underneath it.

For all its simplicity, fan-tan was a game with strict rules and high stakes. Fortunes could be quickly won and lost. Gambling was illegal, but the Chinese knew they could always stay one step ahead of the law.

Fan Tan Alley was narrow, measuring barely one and a half metres wide at both ends, where watchmen stood on guard behind solid wood doors. Entrances to buildings in the wider central section of the alley led to a deliberately confusing maze of connecting rooms, staircases and rooftop escape routes. By the time an officer of the law managed to make an entrance, the gamblers were usually nowhere to be found.

After the end of the Second World War, when rules regarding Chinese immigration were relaxed, many Chinese families arrived, and gambling ceased to be a leisure-time focus. One hundred years after the first Chinese came to Victoria, only one fan-tan house remained. Now there are none.

Chinese men may still like to gamble, but a stroll down Fan Tan Alley today reveals nothing more decadent than retail outlets, galleries, a barbershop and stores. Yet that narrow, brick-lined lane, the unique area surrounding it, and our thriving Chinese community form fascinating links with Victoria's colourful past.

LEE MONG KOW WAY
600-block Fisgard

Opposite the Chinese Public School at 636 Fisgard, just east of Government, is a short lane named for Lee Mong Kow. The school was one of his major accomplishments. But if

⌘ Chinatown has been the setting for many a movie, including *Bird on a Wire*, in which Mel Gibson and Goldie Hawn race through Fan Tan Alley on a motorcycle, with millimetres to spare on either side of the handlebars. The alley once led to opium and gambling dens but now features stores, studios and a barbershop.

Lee were around today, he'd have a hard time believing his eyes. The Chinatown *he* first saw, well over 100 years ago, was a very different Chinatown to the one you're looking at today.

Lee was not yet 30 when he came to Canada in 1882. Putting his social skills and knowledge of English to good use, Lee bridged the gap between the residents of Chinatown and the white population south of Pandora Avenue. By the mid-1880s he had been appointed "interpreter" at the Customs House—the first port of entry for Chinese into Canada. Later he was transferred to the immigration department, where he helped Chinese newcomers cut through the bureaucratic red tape that threatened to strangle them with all its rules and regulations.

Community concerns were his top priority. He was involved with the Chinese Consolidated Benevolent Association and the Lee's Benevolent Association. Convinced that education was the key to a successful future for Chinatown's residents, he helped start a school in the Chinese Consolidated Benevolent Association building. In the early 1900s, when non-English-speaking Chinese-born students were barred from public schools, Lee was instrumental in building the Imperial Chinese School, and he served as its principal for 12 years. Finally, in 1920, the much-honoured Lee retired and moved to Hong Kong. He died there four years later.

By that time the city had crept closer to—and surrounded—Chinatown. City hall, at the corner of Douglas and Pandora, was resplendent in its red-painted glory. Cormorant

Street, originally the centre of Chinatown, was destined to become Centennial Square. But Lee was not forgotten. In 2005, 93-year-old Laura Lai Lee Bow Wah, Lee's 13th child, attended the dedication of the lane that bears her famous father's name and links Fisgard with Centennial Square.

The Chinese Public School still serves the community. At 4 PM each weekday, students walk through its iron gates, just as they did over a century ago. Fresh from their Western curriculum lessons, they come here to continue their education—as Lee Mong Kow would have wished—by keeping their Eastern culture and language alive.

⌘ Jeff Maltby's Chinatown Heritage murals opposite the school show Lee Mong Kow and his family, and children running toward the gate of the school. Other Maltby murals bring the northeast corner of Fisgard and Government to life, while Robert Amos's Dragon Dance mural can be seen high up on the side of the Yen Wo Society building (1713 Government).

PEMBROKE
DISCOVERY
CHATHAM S
HERALD ST.
FISGARD S
PANDORA A
JOHNSON S
YATES ST.
VIEW
FORT ST.
BROUGHTON
COURTNEY S
HUMBOLDT S
Fairmon
Empress
BELLEVILLE
SUPERIOR S
MICHIGAN
TORONTO ST
SIMCOE ST.

⌘ LEFT The Imperial Chinese School, established by the Chinese community in 1909 to teach immigrant children English so they could attend the white schools, was the first Chinese public school in Canada. More than a century later, this school, with its elegant tiled roof and upturned eaves and corners, is a National Historic Site and serves as a cultural centre.

⌘ RIGHT For new arrivals in Chinatown, benevolent associations provided valuable information about the area as well as ideas for places to live and work.

CENTENNIAL SQUARE

Today it's a wide-open space, but yesterday it was Cormorant Street, the centre of Chinatown. This is where, in 1858, the first Chinese merchants conducted business. Twenty years later, Victoria's city hall was built on the south side of Cormorant. On the north side, an ornate 1891 structure housed the main firehall, the Victoria Public Market and the Victoria & Sidney Railway's downtown terminus.

Decades came and went, and in the mid-1950s, after the Depression and two world wars had taken their toll, Cormorant Street was looking the worse for wear. In 1957 city council decided to sell the aging city hall and its adjoining land. The first bit of history to bite the dust was the public market building. Next in line was city hall, which its detractors were determined to replace with a modern city centre.

Fortunately, Richard Biggerstaff Wilson, elected mayor in 1962, had other ideas. You might say that Wilson had a vested interest in preserving history—after all, his grandfather had opened a clothing store on Government Street a century earlier—W. & J. Wilson Clothiers —which was still prospering. R.B. Wilson believed in saving historic structures from the scrap heap. Under his leadership, the feverish rush to replace gave way to renovation and renewal. The historic city hall building was restored and expanded, and Cormorant Street was reinvented as a public meeting place.

On its north side, where the public market building had once stood, a modern multi-level parkade rose above ground-level specialty shops. The old police station, which faces onto Fisgard, received a facelift, as did the McPherson Playhouse. A fountain featuring mosaic concrete totems and a balustraded rim, supposedly reminiscent of Queen Victoria's crown, served as a focal point for Centennial Square—the city's 100th birthday gift to itself.

Before he died in 1991, former mayor Wilson was named to the Order of Canada in recognition of his many and varied accomplishments. Today, Centennial Square serves as a venue for everything from protests to honouring ceremonies, demonstrations to displays of public art, parades to theatre performances, music and cultural festivals to local markets. It's a civic centre, a public gathering place, just as R.B. Wilson intended it to be all those years ago.

CITY HALL
Centennial Square

Standing guard at Centennial Square's southeast corner, Victoria's red-brick city hall is the oldest such municipal building in British Columbia.

It was Roderick Finlayson, former assistant to James Douglas, who as mayor in the late 1870s announced his suggested location for the new civic headquarters. Citizens were amazed. Government Street was only just pushing its way north from Johnson, which

PEMBROKE
DISCOVERY
CHATHAM S
HERALD ST.
FISGARD S
PANDORA A
JOHNSON S
YATES ST.
VIEW
FORT ST.
BROUGHTON
COURTNEY S
HUMBOLDT S
Fairmon
Empress
BELLEVILLE
SUPERIOR S
MICHIGAN
TORONTO S
SIMCOE ST.

⌘ The city hall's clock reached us by a somewhat circuitous route. Manufactured in England in 1881, it was reportedly first sent in error to Victoria, Australia, so was not installed here until 1891.

meant that city hall would be on the outskirts of town. But Mayor Finlayson prevailed. He knew that the fast-growing town would soon catch up to its newest addition.

The building was completed in 1878. In 1881 it was enlarged at its southwest corner to house the fire department, and 10 years later a north wing was added. Former mayor Charles Redfern, who advertised his Government Street jewellery store with a huge clock high above its entrance, won the contract to install the city's civic timepieces.

The clocks, specially ordered from Croydon, England, and installed in 1891, were a sight to behold. Four dials, each two and a half metres in diameter, graced the square tower, and the bell alone weighed more than 950 kilograms. The clocks had to be wound once a week. Fluorescent lights have replaced the gaslights that once illuminated the Roman numerals, but the heavy cast-iron weights are still hand-cranked.

Threatened with demolition more than once over the years, city hall has been extensively renovated and has survived to tell the tale, a symbol of the confidence that Roderick Finlayson had in our city well over a century ago.

THE FIRE BELL This large bronze bell hangs mutely now, its clapper long gone, a relic of a bygone age when bells called people to action when fire broke out.

In 1858 local businessmen, alarmed by the profusion of wooden buildings erected for the township's fast-growing population, petitioned Governor James Douglas for a fire service. The following year the volunteer-run Union Hook and Ladder Company was in operation. By the time Victoria was incorporated as a city three years later, Deluge Engine Company No. 1 and Tiger Engine Company No. 2 had joined the firefighting fray. In 1886 all three volunteer companies disbanded and a paid department was organized. By 1900, Victoria had five firehalls, including one on Cormorant Street (today's Centennial Square) with a watchtower boasting this magnificent 680-kilogram bronze bell, cast in England and purchased for the princely sum of $750.

Today, firefighting is more sophisticated than those long-ago volunteers could ever have imagined. Blaring sirens have taken the place of the bells that once brought men running to haul out the pumpers. The Cormorant Street bell, replaced in 1904 by a more modern telegraphic alarm system, was tucked away in storage and now has pride of place near the Pandora Street entrance to city hall, metres from its original home. It's no longer needed for fires, and on December 31, when nearby bells peal to herald a new year, this old bronze bell stays silent in memory of the brave men who served as firefighters in Victoria's early days.

⌘ One of a chain of theatres built by Greek immigrant Alexander Pantages, the McPherson Playhouse (formerly the Orpheum) features magnificently restored Edwardian decor complete with gilded plaster cherubs, acanthus leaf mouldings, harps and mandolins, and marbled Tuscan columns.

MCPHERSON PLAYHOUSE
Government at Centennial Square

The theatre standing in solitary splendour on the west side of Centennial Square reminds us that long after the first home-grown attempts at entertainment in the Assembly Hall at Fort Victoria, and long before motion pictures made their debut, live theatre was all the rage.

The 986-seat Orpheum Theatre was specially designed for musical theatre and vaudeville. Eva Hart, one of Victoria's most popular singers and actresses, was a featured performer. Nearby, the 480-seat Savoy Theatre's floor was built on a steep incline so that those sitting at the back could see as well as those at the front, and there were no pillars to block anyone's view. Other theatres along Government Street enticed paying audiences with popular stars.

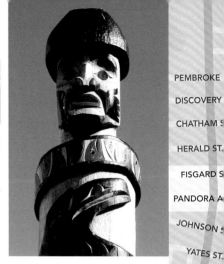

When moving pictures made their debut, many outlets were adapted to accommodate them, and new ones were created. The Majestic Theatre on Lower Yates Street assured a "change of programme three times a week" and proudly proclaimed, "We cater to ladies and children."

The advent of "talkies" spawned movie theatres with names like Dominion (which featured Victoria's first talking picture, Al Jolson's *Sonny Boy*), Empress, Princess, Capitol and Columbia. A few of these old-time entertainment centres remain as retail outlets; many are long since gone. But on Government Street, the McPherson Playhouse, built in 1914 as the Orpheum and now part of Centennial Square, still draws theatregoing crowds, just as it did decades ago. •

⌘ At the southwest entrance to Centennial Square, Two Brothers—Spirit Poles carved by Butch Dick and his sons, Clarence and Bradley—signify a gateway to the land. The poles honour the Songhees and Lekwungen people who, in the days when water flowed through the area, were the first to call this place home.

PEMBROKE

DISCOVERY

CHATHAM S

HERALD ST.

FISGARD S

PANDORA A

JOHNSON S

YATES ST.

VIEW

FORT ST.

BROUGHTON

COURTNEY S

HUMBOLDT S

Fairmon
Empres

BELLEVILLE

SUPERIOR S

MICHIGAN

TORONTO S

SIMCOE ST.

SPIRIT POLES TELL STORIES At different locations around our Inner Harbour and downtown, poles tell stories of the First Nations who called this area home for centuries before the European settlers arrived.

Totem poles can be seen along Government Street from Centennial Square to Dallas Road, on the grounds of the legislature, in parks, on street corners or safely preserved inside the Royal BC Museum. They are a feature of Victoria, yet their origins stem from customs established many kilometres farther north, among nations such as the Haida and Kwakwaka'wakw.

In a culture whose history and traditions are spoken rather than written, totem poles told stories. They took many forms—house posts, story poles, mortuary poles, memorial or commemorative poles. Each one represented the history of a particular clan or family and served as a reminder of its ancestry. Thus each pole became a Tree of Life. These poles were never worshipped; however, early missionaries saw them as pagan idols and destroyed many of them. Others were cut down and shipped to museums all over the world.

A government ban on potlatch ceremonies, or gatherings, which included the raising of totem poles, put an end to the carving of new poles. As time went by, existing poles fell to the ground, as they were meant to do, but now there were no new poles to replace them. This is what inspired Victoria-born artist Emily Carr to travel to First Nation communities on Vancouver Island, the BC mainland and Haida Gwaii to paint the poles before they were lost for all time. In 1951, six years after Emily died, the government ban on potlatches was lifted, and the art form was revived.

At Thunderbird Park beside the Royal BC Museum, in front of the legislature, at the south end of the causeway, in Beacon Hill Park and in Centennial Square—every pole in Victoria tells a story.

Looking south from Fort Street along Government today, it's hard to imagine that Fort Victoria's cedar palisades once marched along the right-hand (west) sidewalk almost to Broughton Street, with the fort's vegetable garden stretching along the left (east) side of the street to halfway between Broughton and Courtney. A walk along this section of Government Street, from Fort to the Inner Harbour, tells us much about the people who lived and worked here in Victoria's early days.

BARD & BANKER SCOTTISH PUB
1020–22 Government

The large cream-coloured building on the southwest corner of Government and Fort has served many different functions. Today it's a popular pub. Yesterday it was a retail store. Way back in the 1880s, it was one of several banks on Government Street—and temporary home to a budding bard.

In the first decade of the 1900s, British-born Robert Service applied to work at the Bank of BC's Government Street branch. He preferred ballads to banking, but he needed a job and somewhere to live. His new post provided him with both; one of the perks of employment was free accommodation on the bank's top floor in return for his services as night watchman.

Less than a year later, Service was transferred, first to Kamloops, then to the Yukon. In Whitehorse he penned a rhyme titled "The Shooting of Dan McGrew." It didn't much please him, so he tucked it away in a desk drawer. His next effort, "The Cremation of Sam McGee," using a name borrowed from a bank ledger, was an instant hit.

Service had no personal experience of the rigours and hardships of the Klondike gold rush, but his romanticized tales in works of poetry and fiction, such as *Rhymes of a Rolling Stone* and *The Trail of Ninety-Eight*, struck a chord with readers everywhere. Publishers could barely keep up with him. This penchant for winning words earned him more in royalties each month than he earned in a year as a bank teller—and probably more than most of the miners he wrote about ever gained in a gold find.

His future assured, Service resigned from the bank and went to France. He married, had a daughter and eventually settled permanently in Monte Carlo. More than 28 novels, poems and autobiographies, including *Songs of*

PEMBROKE
DISCOVERY
CHATHAM
HERALD ST
FISGARD
PANDORA
JOHNSON
YATES ST
VIEW
FORT ST.
BROUGHTON
COURTNEY
HUMBOLDT
Fairmon
Empres
BELLEVILLE
SUPERIOR
MICHIGAN
TORONTO
SIMCOE ST.

⌘ Built in the Renaissance Revival style, the former Bank of British Columbia was built on the site of Fort Victoria's bachelors quarters. The corner entrance is topped by a Greek gable and the likeness of Mercury, the Greek winged god of commerce. The building's grand interior, lovingly restored by local businessman Matt McNeil, is now home to the Bard & Banker pub, named for Robert Service, bard of the Yukon, whose portrait is prominently displayed on an interior wall. In the early 1900s, Service slept in a room on the bank's third floor while serving as night watchman—and some say he haunts the building still.

a Sourdough (later known as *The Spell of the Yukon*), *Ballads of a Cheechako* and *Ploughman of the Moon: An Adventure into Memory*, made him a fortune. In 1958 he died a millionaire.

Service never revisited Victoria, but the grand old building where he worked stands exactly where he left it well over a century ago.

SITE OF THE BROWN JUG SALOON
1023 Government

Today, the small brick edifice opposite the Bard & Banker houses a high-end jewellery store, but several decades ago it was an exclusive hostelry called the Brown Jug Saloon. Considering that its owner, John D. Carroll, lived here for only a few short years, he managed to make quite an impression on Victoria's citizens—and certainly kept them well supplied with beer.

Carroll was an Irishman who came here via California in 1858, lured like so many others by the prospect of a fortune to be found on the Fraser. Arriving in Victoria at the height of gold-rush fever, he set up as a liquor merchant and grocer. Hundreds of men came and went to the goldfields, but Carroll was never tempted to join them. He had spied a golden opportunity of a different sort—a way to augment his walk-in business by offering a sit-down spot where a man could enjoy a drink and a chat with others similarly inclined.

Despite stiff competition from close to two dozen nearby watering holes, the Brown Jug Saloon was a hit from the minute he opened its doors in 1861. Carroll had an interesting edge over his competitors. For one thing, his saloon boasted an elegant glass-and-brass interior; for another, it was the only one serving beer in brown bottles with a label that said "Brown Jug."

Sadly, Carroll's commercial success didn't spill over into his personal life. His first wife, Adele, died soon after their arrival in Victoria, and second wife Ellen lost one baby after another, each within hours of birth. Carroll buried his grief in busy-ness. Along with the store and the saloon, he developed a passenger and freight wagon service between Victoria and Esquimalt, volunteered with the fire department and was an active politician. He had achieved much during his short time here, but in the spring of 1862, before he could reap his rewards, he fell ill. By mid-July he was dead, the victim of consumption.

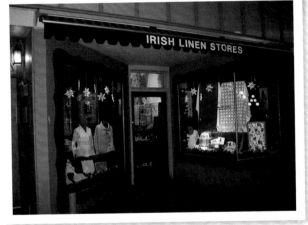

⌘ The Brown Jug Saloon, built by John Carroll in 1861 on the site of the HBC's bakery, was the first watering hole for those travelling south from Fort Street. Carroll was long gone by 1912, when the saloon's owner at the time took over the building next door, known as the Albion Hotel when London-based publisher Thomas Dixon Galpin erected it in 1884. The Galpin Block's ground-floor tenant, the Irish Linen Stores, established by John Norrie, has occupied this sidewalk spot since 1917.

PEMBROKE
DISCOVERY
CHATHAM S
HERALD ST.
FISGARD S
PANDORA A
JOHNSON S
YATES ST.
VIEW
FORT ST.
BROUGHTON
COURTNEY S
HUMBOLDT S
Fairmon
Empres
BELLEVILLE
SUPERIOR S
MICHIGAN
TORONTO S
SIMCOE ST.

The Brown Jug Saloon continued under new ownership, but in 1917, after operating as a pub for 56 years, it bowed to Prohibition and was closed. Much renovated over the ensuing decades, the building retains little of its early history . . . and no hint at all of the Irishman who conducted business here in the heady gold-rush days over 150 years ago.

SITE OF BC FUNERAL FURNISHING CO.
1016 Government

Every new settlement needs someone to provide funeral services, and the young city of Victoria was no exception. Charles Hayward set up his undertaking business on this Government Street spot in 1867.

A carpenter and joiner by trade, Hayward had sailed here intent on finding a fortune in the goldfields so he could rejoin Sarah, his new bride, in England. However, conversations with shipmates convinced the devout teetotaller that gold mining was not for him. Sensibly, he decided to forget about prospecting and pursue his chosen trade.

When the *Sierra Nevada* dropped anchor at Esquimalt in May 1862, Hayward found a small town with part of a Hudson's Bay fur-trading post still standing, and some 1,000 people, many of them permanent residents. Someone with his cabinetmaking skills should do well here . . . and the sooner the better, because he missed his young wife terribly. "I wish dear Sarah was coming in the next vessel," he wrote in his diary.

In October, when he learned that Sarah was on her way, his diary entry was a heady mix of passion and practicality. "I am almost mad with delight at the thought of soon meeting my precious jewel again. Am busy making a bedstead." By mid-January 1863, they were together at last. Sarah's arrival gave Hayward a new lease on life. No more sleeping on the floor with his boots for a pillow. No more lonely nights. His home was furnished, comfortable and filled with love.

It was a small step from cabinets to caskets, and in 1867, Hayward established the BC Funeral Furnishing Company on the west side of Government Street. It was a dream come true. Devout as ever, he gave thanks to his Lord for helping him resist the glitter of gold. Here in Victoria, he had found the recipe for success. People lived; people died. The funeral business would never go out of style.

Speaking of style, Hayward's funerals were a sight to behold. Black horses, plumed and draped in black, pulled black hearses with ornate carvings, silver trim and plate glass. Children's funerals featured white ponies draped in white. In those slower, more respectful times, everything stopped for the solemn, slow-moving procession with its visible symbols of grief.

At the age of 46, the tall, well-groomed Hayward cut quite a figure. He rarely missed a Sunday sermon at the church he had helped build at the foot of Blanshard Street for his friend Bishop Cridge. A member of city council, he held high positions in many local organizations and institutions, even filling the role of chief magistrate. During his term as mayor (1900–1902), one of his many accomplishments was the building of a causeway that permanently linked the busy downtown area to James Bay.

Sadly, Sarah died during his mayoral term. Eighteen years later, Hayward, director of hundreds of funerals, became the centre of his own. It was a splendid affair, one of the largest ever held in Victoria. The solemn procession moved slowly to Ross Bay Cemetery, where Charles Hayward, carpenter-turned-undertaker and full funeral services provider, was finally laid to rest.

SITE OF CHARLES REDFERN'S JEWELLERY STORE
1009 Government

Across Government Street from Charles Hayward's undertaking business, a man with the same first name was advertising expertise of a different sort. Charles Redfern was a jeweller, a Londoner by birth and clockmaker by trade, who arrived here in 1862. Once he saw Victoria, Redfern changed his mind about gold mining in the Cariboo. This was an exciting new city. People had carriages and fine homes—and best of all, there wasn't another clockmaker in sight.

Redfern started up a small jewellery and clockmaking business; by 1875 he had bought out another jeweller and established himself on Government Street. Two years later he was ready to take a bride. Eliza Arden Robinson, also British-born, was 12 years his junior. The two were married in 1877 and lived in James Bay.

By then everyone knew Redfern's downtown store because he had a gimmick that was guaranteed to get attention every minute of every day: a magnificent two-sided clock was suspended above the sidewalk from the second level of the building. Ordered especially from

PEMBROKE
DISCOVERY
CHATHAM S
HERALD ST.
FISGARD S
PANDORA A
JOHNSON S
YATES ST.
VIEW
FORT ST.
BROUGHTON
COURTNEY S
HUMBOLDT S
Fairmon
Empres
BELLEVILLE
SUPERIOR S
MICHIGAN
TORONTO S
SIMCOE ST.

⌘ ABOVE Looking north from Broughton Street toward Fort. Only the wider sidewalks and a profusion of trees separate us from the Government Street of days gone by. Fashions have changed, businesses have changed, but the essence of Government Street remains the same. It is still the city's primary downtown business thoroughfare, whose architecture provides a legacy of long-ago Victoria.

⌘ RIGHT In this photo, looking south from Fort Street in the early 1900s, a street sweeper brushes dust and debris from the streetcar tracks. The unique iron-faced Bank of British Columbia building, not yet painted white, is at near right. Just beyond it, indicated by the dark, rectangular sign, is Hayward's Funeral Services (which continues in business to this day at a different site) and the second-floor studio of Edgar and Harold Fleming, Photographers. On the immediate left in the picture is the single-storey Brown Jug Saloon. Farther down, you can see the large clock hanging over the entrance to Charles Redfern's jewellery store. Beyond it are the large windows of the four-storey Weiler Brothers building. At the end of the street on the right, in the distance, is the second Customs House, long since demolished, which housed both the customs office and a post office.

ent St., Victoria, B. C.

MIRRO
ARTISTS' MA

B. C.
FUNERAL FURNISHING CO. LT?

PEMBROKE
DISCOVERY
CHATHAM S
HERALD ST.
FISGARD S
PANDORA A
JOHNSON S
YATES ST.
VIEW
FORT ST.
BROUGHTON
COURTNEY S
HUMBOLDT S
Fairmon
Empres
BELLEVILLE
SUPERIOR S
MICHIGAN S
TORONTO S
SIMCOE ST.

England, Victoria's first town clock remained a wonder for decades to come.

Redfern became the city's 15th mayor in 1883. In 1891 he installed Victoria's most famous clock—the one at city hall. In 1899 he was responsible for the purchase of a new, state-of-the-art steam pumper for fighting fires. What a sight it was! It took two horses to hurtle the *Charles E. Redfern* through the downtown streets. Handsomely finished with Russian iron lagging, heavy brass spun bands and a nickel dome, it could achieve 100 p.s.i. in just over 10 minutes and throw a single stream of water over 70 metres.

In the first two decades of the new century, Redfern's fortunes changed. His beloved wife died. During the economic downturn preceding the First World War, his business went bankrupt. He retired in 1922 and died seven years later, after suffering a stroke in his 89th year. The fire engine named in his honour, restored to its former glory and preserved for posterity, is still a firm favourite in downtown parades. The city hall timepiece ticks on without him, and the building that housed his jewellery store—minus its magnificent clock—stands on Government Street to this day.

⌘ In this view looking west toward the harbour, the deep-pink building with the mansard-style roof at the foot of Broughton Street on Wharf Street is Victoria's first Customs House. Built in 1874 on what had once been Fort Victoria's southwest corner, the Customs House signalled the end of Victoria's days as a free port. It was the first federal building west of Ontario—one of the "carrots" dangled by the Dominion government to help entice British Columbia into Confederation. (The other "carrot"—a transcontinental railroad—took a lot longer to build and never did get as far as Victoria.) In the days before home delivery of mail, the Customs House served as the main post office, and in the 1890s was the licence-issuing office for gold miners headed to the Klondike. From 1954 to 1964, it was home to HMCS *Malahat*, Canada's oldest naval division.

PEMBERTON BUILDING
1000 Government

Joseph Despard Pemberton, founder of the company that once had its headquarters in this building, laid out the plan for the Victoria township and surrounding area over 150 years ago.

Pemberton was an Irish-born surveyor and engineer who in 1850 learned that the London-based Hudson's Bay Company planned to colonize Vancouver Island and was looking for a qualified surveyor. He applied and was immediately accepted. James Douglas eagerly awaited his arrival. Two years earlier, the British government had leased Vancouver Island to the HBC for the princely sum of seven shillings a year (about three dollars in today's money), with the proviso that the company must attract significant British settlement. Douglas was anxious to keep his part of the bargain, and Pemberton was up for the challenge.

Pemberton sailed into Esquimalt Harbour in 1851. Within four months, he and his assistant, Benjamin William Pearse, had completed a preliminary survey of Vancouver Island's coastline and mapped out the HBC land surrounding Fort Victoria. Pemberton's town plan included schools and churches. The rolling meadows and forested areas that Douglas had earlier earmarked for public use became Beacon Hill Park. Government Street—named for the small residence built for Governor Richard Blanshard—became the first official street west of the Rockies in British North America.

His plan for the townsite completed in 1852, Pemberton went on to supervise construction of roads, bridges, lighthouses, law courts and the new seat of colonial government, in which he proudly served as a member of the legislative assembly. In the mid-1880s he built a grand new home on his vast estate in Oak Bay, where he and his elegant, aristocratic wife Teresa entertained on a grand scale.

Toward the end of the 1880s, Pemberton and his son Frederick started up in business

PEMBROKE
DISCOVERY
CHATHAM S
HERALD ST.
FISGARD S
PANDORA AV
JOHNSON S
YATES ST.
VIEW
FORT ST.
BROUGHTON
COURTNEY S
HUMBOLDT S
Fairmon
Empress
BELLEVILLE S
SUPERIOR S
MICHIGAN S
TORONTO ST
SIMCOE ST.

downtown. In 1893, Joseph Pemberton suffered a massive heart attack and died, leaving 28-year-old Fred in full charge of the business. Fred's son-in-law, Cuthbert Holmes, joined him, and in 1947, Pemberton Holmes Realtors opened an office on the northwest corner of Government and Broughton. Their new home was in a building constructed in 1899 by Charles A. Vernon of the BC Pottery Company on the site of old Fort Victoria, where Joseph Despard Pemberton's illustrious Victoria career had begun a century earlier. Pemberton Holmes Realtors thrives in Victoria to this day.

⌘ Looking north from Courtney Street in 1909. On the left is the West End Grocery, on the main floor of the building that later housed the offices of Pemberton Holmes Realtors. The Bank of Montreal's chateau-style roof can be seen in the distance. In the centre of the picture, there is little motorized traffic to hinder the cyclists or the streetcar. The striped awnings above the Weiler Brothers' showroom windows can be seen in the right foreground. On the next corner is the Hamley Building, built for Wymond Hamley, collector of customs from 1864 to 1871 and a member of the legislative assembly. Beyond it, Redfern's clock hangs high above pedestrians on the east sidewalk. This whole block was built on the site of Fort Victoria's vegetable garden.

WEILER BUILDING
921 Government

The first thing that strikes you about the building on the southeast corner of Government and Broughton is its unusually styled windows. On the upper floor, they are deep—twice as deep, in fact, as the interior area they're designed to illuminate. These were the showroom premises for John Weiler, first in his family to supply furnishings for Victoria's finer homes.

Like many others, Weiler was enticed here by the prospect of making money as a gold miner and stock rancher. Born in Germany in 1824, he came to Victoria via California with his wife, Christiana, and their four children. Originally Cariboo-bound, Weiler was sidetracked by the promise of even better pickings in Victoria, a newly incorporated city eager to move beyond its HBC beginnings. Fort Victoria was as good as gone. In its place, businesses and homes were popping up—and they all needed furniture.

Weiler opened a modest upholstery and furniture store. It did so well that by the early 1880s, John Weiler, Upholsterer & Paperhanger, was selling everything from oilcloth and carpets to cornices and window blinds, from mattresses and lounge sets to crockery and cutlery. Soon, the brick "warerooms" on Broad Street couldn't cope with the demand. In 1899, Weiler Brothers Home Furnishings stood ready in a substantial new building on Government Street to serve its customers.

By this time, John Weiler had handed the business over to his four sons and was enjoying a leisurely retirement. The firm continued under the family name until the early 1930s.

Today, visitors to Craigdarroch Castle can still see a chest of drawers bearing the Weiler company's brass nameplate, and a tiny china tea cup bearing the castle's likeness, made by special order in Austria. And on the southeast corner of Government and Broughton Streets, the sturdy stone Weiler building with the impressive arched windows stands as tall and as proud as it did when John Weiler watched it being built well over a century ago.

⌘ OPPOSITE TOP This 1907 aerial view north, probably taken from the roof of the Weiler Building at Government and Courtney Streets, shows some interesting features of the growing city. The roof of the building housing the West End Grocery (and, later, the Pemberton Holmes office) can be seen at lower left. Next is Fleming Brothers, Photographers. Directly above their rooftop, a few blocks away, is the provincial courthouse in Bastion Square. The Bank of British Columbia stands on the corner of Fort Street. Above it, you can see the tower of the Oriental Hotel on Yates Street.

Government Street, Victoria, B. C.

2185

⌘ **LEFT** Weiler's showroom carried every conceivable household item. Imported glassware and silverware gleamed in the light from the huge arched windows. An elevator whisked shoppers from floor to floor. The company's 350-page catalogue advertised an upholstered chesterfield sofa covered in chintz or taffeta for under $100. A chair covered in Spanish leather cost just $60. Oak and silver butter dishes were $2 each. Among the many fine homes furnished by Weiler's was James Dunsmuir's Craidgdarroch Castle, completed in 1899. Check the sidewalk at the southeast corner of Government and Fort for a plaque indicating a distant view of the castle atop the Fort Street hill.

73

PEMBROKE S
DISCOVERY
CHATHAM S
HERALD ST.
FISGARD S
PANDORA A
JOHNSON S
YATES ST.
VIEW
FORT ST.
BROUGHTON
COURTNEY S
HUMBOLDT S
Fairmon
Empress
BELLEVILLE S
SUPERIOR ST
MICHIGAN S
TORONTO ST
SIMCOE ST.

ROGERS' CHOCOLATES
913 Government

The plaque in the sidewalk outside Rogers' Chocolates tells us something of what went on in the building beside us, but very little about the man who owned it. Charles Rogers, one of downtown's most successful entrepreneurs, certainly knew how to tickle the taste buds of his faithful followers. Yet his story is an interesting mix of success and sadness.

Hailing originally from Massachusetts, Rogers came to Victoria in 1885 at the age of 31. He set up a greengrocery on the west side of Government Street but before long recognized a more lucrative opportunity. Carefully combining his fruits with the finest, freshest ingredients, he created chocolate-covered combinations that, to this day, no one else has quite been able to match.

The enterprising Charles married local lass Leah Morrison in 1888. They set up home in James Bay and two years later welcomed a son, Frederick. Business on Government Street was booming, but there wasn't much sweetness and light in the Rogers household. Young Fred showed no interest in the candy-making business. Instead, much to his parents' dismay, he developed a morbid fascination with explosives. In 1905 tragedy struck twice. Fred lost three fingers in an explosives-related accident. Then he rented a room at the New England Hotel and, after writing a note to his parents, shot himself to death.

Grief-stricken, Charles and Leah buried themselves in their work. Rising early and working late, Charles often sold all the chocolates he had made the previous day within an hour. Then the shop door was closed. The afternoons were devoted to filling mail orders, for Rogers' chocolates were now being shipped all over the world.

Needing more space, Rogers moved his business into a two-storey block that he owned across the street. The main floor, previously rented by a jewellery store, had ample display space up front, while the back portion was adapted to become a miniature chocolate-making factory. Charles delighted in buying expensive gifts for Leah, and nothing pleased him more than to have her don her furs and diamonds and sit with him as he worked through the evening.

When Charles died of a heart attack in 1927 at the age of 73, he left an estate worth almost $300,000—a veritable fortune at that time. Leah donated money to charities, made poor investments and gradually lost everything

that Charles had left her. When she died in 1952 at the age of 88, she was living on an old-age pension.

Rogers' Chocolates is still locally owned and operated. The old-fashioned glass-topped entrance door, curved glass jewellery-display counters filled with chocolates, and the floor tiles spelling out his family name are exactly where Charles Rogers left them, all those years ago.

SITE OF THE WINDSOR HOTEL
901 Government

Today it houses retail stores, but 150 years ago, George Richardson's Windsor Hotel, on the corner of Government and Courtney, was our city's first all-brick hostelry.

⌘ Outside Victoria's favourite chocolate store, a sidewalk plaque commemorates one of Government Street's best-known businesses. Inside, high on the wall, a framed portrait of Charles and Leah Rogers reminds us of the couple who tasted bittersweet success on the Government Street of days gone by. Today, Rogers' Chocolates is a store for all seasons, with a mail-order business that spreads its goodness worldwide.

PEMBROKE
DISCOVERY
CHATHAM S
HERALD ST.
FISGARD S
PANDORA A
JOHNSON S
YATES ST.
VIEW
FORT ST.
BROUGHTON
COURTNEY S
HUMBOLDT S
Fairmon
Empres
BELLEVILLE
SUPERIOR S
MICHIGAN
TORONTO S
SIMCOE ST.

⌘ Minus the impressive, high-arched brick entrance that once enticed travellers through its doors, and with its sturdy brick construction hidden behind a decades-old mock-Tudor frontage, the former Windsor Hotel is now home to retail outlets.

The 23-year-old Richardson arrived at Fort Victoria to work for the Hudson's Bay Company in the early spring of 1850. By the end of that decade he had bought land, found himself a British bride, and built a fine hotel not far from the wooden bridge that led to the new home of the legislative assembly. Richardson was justifiably proud of his building, but early one morning in 1876 he almost destroyed it.

It was Mary Ann Richardson who smelled the gas first. Alarmed, she woke her sleeping husband, who went downstairs to investigate . . . carrying a lighted candle to help him find his way. The resulting explosion, which was allegedly heard clear out to Oak Bay, blew down brick partitions, tore plaster from walls, wrenched doors from frames and wrecked the parlour and dining room. Ignited gas rushed up the stairwell and blew out windows, littering the street below with shattered glass. Amazingly, no one was seriously hurt. Richardson suffered severely singed hair, a burned hand and hurt pride, but he lived to tell the tale—and to repair the damage to his precious building.

George Richardson died in 1922 at the ripe old age of 96. Today, the former Windsor Hotel is a legacy of another era, and a memorial to the proud proprietor of Victoria's first all-brick hotel.

BELMONT BUILDING
600 Humboldt at Government

The Belmont Building, on the northeast corner of Government and Humboldt Streets, is a fine example of the city's confidence in its future during the first decade of the 1900s. An economic upswing had fostered an unprecedented building boom, and, one by one, solid, tall structures took the place of the smaller buildings that preceded them.

The Belmont Saloon had stood on this site for some 30 years. Its owner, Thomas Flewin,

came to Victoria in 1853 to work for the HBC. In the 1880s he switched from warehousing to watering holes and bought two saloons, including one on Government Street at the corner of Humboldt. With a dance hall right next door, his business was well placed to succeed. But with the turn of the century, times were changing. Now the saloon was to be knocked down and replaced by a modern structure bearing the same name.

Placed to command a splendid view of the Inner Harbour, the Belmont Hotel wasn't even finished when it became a victim of the pre–First World War economic slump. By the time the hotel was completed, at the end of the war, it faced stiff competition from the Empress, and the Belmont's owners decided to refit it as an office block.

⌘ Looking north from the Empress Hotel toward Humboldt Street in the 1920s, a streetcar approaches the Causeway from Government Street on the left, between the old Post Office (long since demolished) and the Belmont Building. On top of the Belmont Building, there's a little hut with a small window and a hip-style roof. This time-ball house was designed to let ships' masters rate their chronometers without leaving their vessels, ensuring they conformed to Greenwich Mean Time. Each day at 12:45 PM, the operator slowly raised the time-ball to the top of a mast. At 1 PM precisely, a land-telegraph signal from the Gonzales Observatory, a few kilometres away, triggered a mechanism that allowed the time-ball to move slowly downward. On the causeway, men with pocket watches in hand gazed upward; out on the strait, ships' masters carefully focused telescopes; everyone waited patiently for the ball to drop. Eventually, over the decades, modern technology took over. The time-ball mast is gone, but the simple cabin stands there still, a reminder that at a certain hour here in Victoria, a good time—or at least the right time—was had by all.

PEMBROKE
DISCOVERY
CHATHAM S
HERALD ST.
FISGARD ST.
PANDORA A
JOHNSON S
YATES ST.
VIEW
FORT ST.
BROUGHTON
COURTNEY S
HUMBOLDT S
Fairmon
Empress
BELLEVILLE
SUPERIOR S
MICHIGAN
TORONTO ST
SIMCOE ST.

⌘ As you walk along the west side of Government Street toward the Inner Harbour, it's a treat to look up and see two huge, colourful murals side by side on the back of the Belmont Building. Vancouver Island artist Tom Brudenell's stunning artwork has graced the building's north wall since 1973. The mural on the right—the one most easily visible from Government Street—features an arbutus tree and the mirror-like waters of the Juan de Fuca Strait. The mural on the left, visible closer to Courtney Street, focuses on the Saanich Peninsula's farmlands and orchards. Both paintings feature as a backdrop the majestic mountains of the Olympic Peninsula in Washington State.

Today the Belmont, retaining its Edwardian elegance, proudly anchors the south end of downtown Government Street overlooking the Inner Harbour. ●

Rarely is a city's waterfront area so completely dominated by a single architect, yet many of the major buildings around you testify to the prowess of one man—Francis Mawson Rattenbury. In the few short decades between his debut on the Victoria scene and his untimely departure from it, Rattenbury had a hand in creating several splendid Inner Harbour structures.

The legislature was the first of the projects to be sketched by the young, Yorkshire-born architect, who beat out more than 60 other contestants with his sweeping design. Shaped like a short-stemmed T, with smaller side buildings and a south wing attached, the centre block is crowned by a copper dome supporting a gilded statue of Captain George Vancouver, after whom this island is named. The Haddington Island stone facade of the building—and Captain Vancouver's statue—are lit up each evening by thousands of light bulbs.

East of the causeway, Rattenbury's Empress Hotel stands on reclaimed land, where once the harbour waters flowed under the old James Bay Bridge. Resting on a concrete platform and supported by Douglas fir pilings driven into the clay, the Empress, which opened in 1908, sports the same chateau-style roof as the old Bank of Montreal on Government Street—another Rattenbury creation. The hotel's centre section sports English ivy, which grows deep-green against its dark red brick, and Boston ivy, a sight to behold when the leaves change colour in the fall. A photograph showing the handsome, debonair Rattenbury in his younger days is displayed between the elevators on the hotel's lower level.

In full view of the Empress, the Greek-temple-style Canadian Pacific Steamship Terminal arose on the waterfront in 1924. Daylight gleams off its Newcastle Island stone-mixed-with-cement surface, and massive columns adorn its reinforced concrete frame. Likenesses of the sea god Poseidon flank the main entrance. With his usual arrogance and enthusiasm, Rattenbury took all the glory for the design of the colonnaded edifice, much to the disgust of colleague Percy L. James, who had actually prepared the drawings and specifications and supervised construction.

Rattenbury rode high on his success for some years, but his star began to tarnish when

CHATHAM

HERALD S

FISGARD

PANDOR

JOHNSON

YATES ST

WHARF ST.

FORT ST

BROUGHT

COURTN

HUMBOLD

Inner
Harbour

BELLEVILLE

SUPERIOR

MICHIGAN S

TORONTO ST

SIMCOE ST.

he conducted a very public affair with the beautiful young pianist at the Empress Hotel. He divorced his first wife, remarried and left the city for good in 1930. Within five years he was dead—murdered by his second wife's younger lover and buried without fanfare in an English churchyard. Victoria's designer darling had become the architect of his own demise.

In 1987 his rise to glory and gradual fall from grace was recreated in a movie titled *Cause Célèbre*, based on Terrence Rattigan's 1977 play by the same name and starring Helen Mirren as Alma, Rattenbury's second wife.

CHATHAM
HERALD S
FISGARD
PANDORA
JOHNSON
YATES ST
WHARF ST.
FORT ST
BROUGHT
COURTN
HUMBOLD
Inner
Harbour
BELLEVILLE
SUPERIOR
MICHIGAN S
TORONTO ST
SIMCOE ST.

⌘ OPPOSITE Looking south over the Inner Harbour in this peaceful 1930s scene, you can see the house built by Victoria entrepreneur David Spencer just to the left at the end of the causeway. The Legislative Buildings are front and centre against the backdrop of Washington State's Olympic Peninsula mountains, and the Canadian Pacific Steamship Terminal is at right.

⌘ ABOVE Today, the scene is much more active but still recognizable. Wharves on the Lower Causeway serve a variety of craft, including Harbour Ferries (inset), kayaks, sailboats, powerboats and the wooden-hulled vessels that attend the annual Classic Boat Festival each September.

⌘ TOP Throughout the summer, Ship Point is alive with tall-masted sailing ships, night markets and entertainment. Float planes at the nearby terminal connect Victoria with Vancouver, Seattle and points Up-Island. Beyond them to the west, Laurel Point and the Songhees mark the Inner Harbour entrance, with the Sooke Hills on the horizon.

⌘ BOTTOM On the plaza behind the Visitor Centre, *The Home-coming* commemorates 100 years of the Canadian Navy's presence in Victoria. In 1909 the Canadian Navy took over from Britain's Royal Navy, which had protected our harbour and coast since the 1860s. The sculpture, which shows a serviceman being greeted by his child, is the work of local artist Nathan Scott, who immortalized his own young daughter in the work. Elsewhere on the plaza, Scott's likeness of Canadian Navy veteran John Mason sits silently on a bench overlooking the water. And at Mile Zero on Dallas Road, the western end of the Trans-Canada Highway, Scott's statue of one-legged Canadian hero Terry Fox, who died after attempting a cross-Canada fundraising run, is shown reaching his goal—the Pacific Ocean—after all.

VISITOR INFORMATION CENTRE
812 Wharf at Government

In its prominent corner spot, the vibrant, flower-bedecked Visitor Centre gives little hint of its practical, decades-old purpose. Yet, on closer inspection, the huge picture windows and large square entrance on the lower level betray the building's humble beginnings—as an Imperial Oil gas station.

In architectural terms, this building can't compare to the other stately structures around the harbour. Francis Rattenbury, architect of the provincial legislature and the Empress Hotel, originally planned another of his dashing designs to grace this side of the harbour. However, he had left Victoria, his reputation in tatters, by the time a building unlike any he could have dreamed of appeared at the north end of the causeway.

The year was 1931. Ten years after the end of the First World War, the city was struggling through a Depression, so the latest addition to our waterfront was a sensible, no-nonsense affair. The lower level served as a repair shop. The middle level provided storage for 120 cars. The upper storey, at street level, was a service station, its California-style pantiled roof fitting Victoria's tourist image of the time as a Palm Springs-type "land of the sun" resort.

The 24-metre, Art Deco-style, stepped tower atop the building sported a revolving beacon at its peak. The 10-million-candle-power light, visible 100 kilometres away, was a bold, forward-looking sign of the times. The First World War had spurred major technological advances and changed the face of business. Aircraft could carry letters and packages farther and faster, and business owners, long held ransom by shipping lines and railways, jumped on the bandwagon. There was only one snag: in order to beat trains and ships at their own game, you had to operate at night, which meant finding a way to guide a small airplane to its destination in the dark.

Enter Elmer Ambrose Sperry. Born in New York in 1860, Sperry channelled his technical abilities into research and development and became one of the most prolific and capable inventors in American history. Included among his successes were a gyrocompass, arc lighting, and a stabilizer and automatic pilot for airplanes. He adapted many of his wartime inventions for peacetime use. One—a searchlight invented for anti-aircraft warfare—was used as a beacon

for the airmail service that was changing the way business was done all over the world.

Sperry's beacons, placed so that pilots flying at low altitudes could see them flashing just above the horizon, marked flight paths and made it possible for small, flimsy-looking airplanes to fly at night. Let's put Victoria on the map, said local businessmen, by establishing a seaplane base in our Inner Harbour. And what better location for a guiding light than the top of the new Imperial Oil garage?

Alas, Sperry's beacon mechanism was obsolete almost before it was switched on. Not that it really mattered. The Inner Harbour seaplane base was a non-starter. Sea captains, seeing it as a threat, campaigned vigorously against the base in its originally envisaged form. Long before the 1930s came to an

⌘ The beacon on top of the Visitor Centre's tower was put there in 1931 to help guide night-flying float planes—a newfangled notion at the time—into our harbour. Today, Victoria's harbour is home to the busiest float plane service in Canada. The clock below the beacon was a gift from Morioka, Victoria's sister city in Japan. In that city's Iwate Park, a totem created by Kwakwaka'wakw master carver Tony Hunt stands on the appropriately named Victoria Road.

end, the only person making money at the Causeway Garage was a fellow by the name of William Wilbey. Born here in 1862, the year Victoria was incorporated as a city, Wilbey ran a taxi service out of the garage until he died in 1940. The service station closed in 1974, and a year later the building was acquired by the province.

Today, the garage and its gas pumps are a distant memory. Most people who push through the Visitor Centre's doors don't even think about the building's origins. But if you stand outside on the deck and look up, you'll see letters running down the side of the tower, beneath the paint, that spell out "Imperial Oil." And on the pinnacle's peak, a modern-day version of Elmer Sperry's revolving beacon still lights the skies every evening.

SHIP POINT

The old and the new . . . Today, visitors arrive at our harbour on motor vessels such as the Black Ball Line's MV *Coho* or the *Clipper*, or on a float plane. But yesterday, everyone arrived by sail or steam on a vessel similar to the black-and-white side-paddlewheeler shown on the next page that was formerly anchored at Ship Point. (It was sold in 2012

to be restored to go on display farther north on Vancouver Island.)

The SS *Beaver*, built on London's River Thames in 1833 as a trading vessel for the Hudson's Bay Company, was the first steamship on the Pacific Northwest coast in the late 1830s. In 1843 she brought James Douglas and his men here to establish Fort Victoria. She ferried people and products up and down the coast before being used as a survey ship until 1874, when she was sold to the first of several owners. In 1888 the *Beaver* foundered on the rocks off Vancouver's Stanley Park at high tide and could not be refloated. There she stayed, high and dry, until 1892, when the wash of another steamship dislodged her and she sank.

In Fort Victoria's early days, HBC ships similar in size to the *Beaver* brought new employees, mostly men, here from the British Isles. Contracted by the HBC to be farm workers, carpenters and general labourers, they worked long and hard for five years, sending for their families and buying land from the HBC once their contracts were complete.

As you look at this 101-foot-long replica, it's hard to imagine the conditions endured by passengers on the HBC's transatlantic vessels, which often carried dozens of men,

CHATHAM
HERALD S
FISGARD
PANDOR
JOHNSON
YATES ST
WHARF ST.
FORT ST
BROUGHT
COURTN
HUMBOLD
Inner Harbour
BELLEVILLE
SUPERIOR
MICHIGAN S
TORONTO ST
SIMCOE ST.

women and children, as well as 30 or so crew members. Depending on weather, their arduous journey across the Atlantic, around Cape Horn and up the west coast might take as long as six months. Once they arrived at Victoria, their ship would anchor in the harbour, and passengers and crew were ferried ashore in rowboats that tied up to the mooring rings still visible in the rocks below the Customs House on Wharf Street.

LEKWUNGEN MARKERS
Lower Causeway

Seven striking pieces of bronze art in and around Victoria's harbour are solid reminders of the original custodians of this land—the Lekwungen, known today as the Esquimalt and Songhees Nations.

When the HBC's James Douglas stepped ashore here in 1842, he saw the result of the Lekwungen people's careful land management, which included controlled burning and food cultivation. The Lekwungen had hunted and gathered here for thousands of years, and the area was a resource-rich trading centre for a diversity of First Peoples.

The Lekwungen helped the HBC men build Fort Victoria and cut down the cedars for the pickets that surrounded it. They watched as the small settlement became a commercial centre, then a provincial capital, and they mourned as the hills, creeks and marshlands they had known and cared for slowly disappeared. It's impossible to experience the landscape the Lekwungen knew all those years ago. However, an innovative project has helped us know more about their traditions and their way of life.

In 2005 the federal government recognized Victoria as a Canadian cultural capital and provided funding for a self-guided, interpretive walkway in and around the Inner Harbour that would promote the artistic, historical and cultural contributions of the Coast Salish people. Local Coast Salish artist Butch Dick was nominated by the Esquimalt and Songhees Nations to carve seven enlarged spindle whorls—small discs used traditionally for spinning wool—to be used as historical markers. The whorls mark places of special importance to the Lekwungen people. Four of the seven are on or near Government Street. Tracing a route from one to the other is a wonderful way to learn about this land, its culture and the spirit of its people. Here's where you'll find those four markers, with a brief description of their significance:

LOWER CAUSEWAY (*xwsɜ yqʼəm*—"*place of mud*") This spindle whorl marks what used to be a tidal mud flat with some of the best clam beds on the coast—which were lost when the area was filled in for construction of the causeway and the Empress Hotel. This was also one end of a canoe portage that led from the eastern edge of today's Ross Bay Cemetery, enabling paddlers to avoid the harbour entrance during heavy seas.

ROYAL BC MUSEUM (*qʼemasənj*) The spindle whorl in front of the Musuem refers to the three nations of Vancouver Island— the Kwakwaka'wakw, Nuu-chah-nulth and Coast Salish. The theme of this carving is "celebrate diversity" and it also evokes the diversity of natural and human histories within the museum.

WHARF PARK (*opposite the foot of Broughton Street*) In the early 1840s, the HBC's Fort Victoria was built on this waterfront. Lekwungen men and women helped build the fort in exchange for trade goods. As the settlement grew, a large forested area around the fort was destroyed, forcing a dramatic change in traditional ways and sustainable land use.

CITY HALL (*on Pandora*—*skwcʼənjiɫc*—"*bitter cherry tree*") Willow-lined, berry-rich creeks once flowed from the food-gathering areas now contained by Fort, View, Vancouver and Quadra Streets, down through present-day Centennial Square

and Market Square and into the harbour. The Lekwungen harvested bark from the bitter cherry trees in the area for use in everyday objects.

All seven original cedar carvings are displayed in the foyers of the city hall.

CPR STEAMSHIP TERMINAL
470 Belleville Street

Adding a touch of classic Greek elegance to the waterfront, the Canadian Pacific Steamship Terminal dates from the days when tall-funnelled ships carrying passengers from all over the world sailed into Victoria's harbour. The colonnaded edifice, complete with twin images of the Greek sea god Poseidon above its entrance, was unveiled to an admiring public

in 1924. Today, the terminal is part of a major redevelopment designed to enhance our waterfront and welcome visitors to our city.

STATUE OF QUEEN VICTORIA
Belleville Street

Faithfully, once a year, we celebrate the birthday of a monarch who never set foot on our shores. She gave our city its name but didn't grace us with her presence. Who *was* Victoria, and why didn't she visit, not even for a cup of tea? The answers are many and complex.

In 1837, when the Hudson's Bay Company started serious exploration of America's west coast, the 18-year-old Princess Victoria was about to ascend to the throne. A year later she was crowned Queen of England. By the time the HBC established its Pacific Northwest headquarters here in 1843, the 24-year-old Victoria was the wife of Prince Albert of Saxe-Coburg and Gotha and the mother of a son and two daughters.

Fifteen years later, when a new name was needed for the territory north of the 49th parallel, it was Queen Victoria who proposed "British Columbia." She was now the mother of nine. The family spent much of its time at Osborne House on the Isle of Wight.

Then, in 1861, the queen's beloved husband—still a young man—died of typhoid fever. Devastated, Victoria went into deep mourning, and from that time on rarely appeared at court ceremonials. But she never neglected her duties as queen and was diligent in her recognition of colonists who served her well. Several prominent Victoria citizens, after a visit to Buckingham Palace, assumed the title "Sir." James Douglas and Matthew Baillie Begbie were among those whose shoulders felt the weight of the ceremonial sword during Queen Victoria's reign.

Why didn't Victoria visit Victoria? In truth, the notion of a royal visit to merely see and be seen had not occurred to the court. Whole portions of the British Empire—even of her own country—never had the pleasure

⌘ Unlike many other statues around the world depicting Queen Victoria in her later years, when she was famously "not amused," the statue in front of our legislature represents a young woman in the prime of life. English sculptor Albert Bruce-Joy was disappointed when his work was not placed near the legislature's entrance, as he had hoped, but closer to Belleville Street, where it is much photographed by hundreds of visitors every year.

CHATHAM S

HERALD S

FISGARD S

PANDORA

JOHNSON

YATES ST.

WHARF ST.

FORT ST.

BROUGHT

COURTNE

HUMBOLD

Inner
Harbour

BELLEVILLE S

SUPERIOR S

MICHIGAN S

TORONTO ST

SIMCOE ST.

of playing host to their monarch. She disliked train travel, and prolonged sea travel made her sick. She studied weather forecasts with care and refused to set sail on a Friday.

This mistrust of the sea was one reason she didn't venture far. In any case, a journey across the Atlantic was deemed unwise because the country on the other side of the 49th parallel was in a state of unrest. By the time the American Civil War was over, Victoria felt she was too old to undertake the long sea voyage.

The queen loved Scotland but visited few parts of England, Ireland and Wales. Most of her relatives were in Europe. She went there often and was particularly fond of the South of France. In fact, a spring holiday was being planned when she fell ill at Osborne House soon after Christmas 1900. A few weeks later, as she lay desperately ill, she apparently raised herself slightly from her pillows and said, "Oh, if I were only at Nice, I should recover."

But it wasn't to be. A few hours later, the 82-year-old Queen of the British Isles and Empress of India, whose name—and likeness—would live on in the city she never saw, was dead. Memorial services were held throughout the world, but according to the *Colonist* newspaper, nowhere in the British Empire were they more universally respected and observed than in Victoria, the Vancouver Island city that bore the monarch's name.

LEGISLATIVE BUILDINGS
Belleville at Government

The provincial legislature was the first imposing Rattenbury-designed structure to grace our Inner Harbour. Opened in February 1898, it had taken five years to complete at a cost almost double the amount budgeted. The interior, roof and facade feature local woods, bricks, slate and stone, as well as other hardwoods, marble, mosaics and stained glass imported from all over the world, along with art commissioned by European-trained artists and sculptors. On either side of the main entrance, larger-than-life likenesses of Chief Justice Sir Matthew Baillie Begbie and Governor James Douglas cast their stony gaze over the parades and protests that regularly take place on the steps at their feet.

At night the building is illuminated by more than 3,000 light bulbs, first switched on in 1897 to celebrate Queen Victoria's jubilee (60 years on the British throne), and augmented by green and red lights at Christmastime.

⌘ On Canada Day (July 1), hundreds of happy people form a "human flag" on the lawn of the BC Legislature while Government Street sparkles with music and entertainment.

⌘ ABOVE LEFT   Looking toward the front of the Legislative Buildings, the bronze cenotaph created by sculptors Vernon and Sidney March of Farnborough, Kent, who later created the National War Memorial in Ottawa, is on the left at the Government Street corner.

⌘ ABOVE CENTRE   At the Belleville Street end of the centre path leading to the legislature's entrance, Albert Bruce-Joy's Queen Victoria (see page 89) surveys the scene from her plinth beside the sequoia that serves as our Christmas Tree.

⌘ LEFT AND ABOVE RIGHT   Near the western corner of the grounds is the Knowledge Pole, created by master carver Cicero August and his sons Darrell and Doug, all members of the Cowichan tribe. The loon, fisherman, bone game player and frog carved into the pole represent lessons of the past and hope for the future.

CHATHAM
HERALD ST
FISGARD S
PANDORA
JOHNSON
YATES ST.
WHARF ST.
FORT ST
BROUGHTO
COURTNE
HUMBOLDT
Inner Harbour
BELLEVILLE S
SUPERIOR S
MICHIGAN ST
TORONTO ST.
SIMCOE ST.

THE EAGLE
(Kwaknul Nootka Sound)

Vancouver Island first occupied for Britain
by Captain James Cook in 1778, became a
centre for the fur trade.
Named after Captain George Vancouver, the
Crown Colony of Vancouver Island was
established in 1849 a fortress British
community on the West Coast.
In 1851 representative government was
instituted and a Legislative Assembly elected.
It was united with the mainland colony of
British Columbia in 1866.

⌘ OPPOSITE The Legislative Library, added to the main building and completed in 1916, features so many stone effigies of famous figures from British Columbia's early history that they have to be identified by a "who's who" explanatory plaque at ground level. At the south end of the grounds, near Superior Street, Robert Savory's Centennial Fountain, celebrating the 1862 union of four territories to form the Colony of British Columbia, has at its centre otters and gulls, symbolizing the fur trade and the sea. Around its rim, the four territories are represented by a bronze-cast eagle (Vancouver Island), raven (Haida Gwaii—formerly the Queen Charlotte Islands), wolf (Stikine) and bear (mainland British Columbia).

⌘ ABOVE Viennese sculptor Frank Cizek's gilded effigy of Britain's Captain George Vancouver has capped the centre dome of the Francis Rattenbury-designed legislature since its completion in 1897. That same year, more than 3,000 electric light bulbs were installed around the outline of the building to celebrate Queen Victoria's Jubilee. When the electrical crew drilled a hole in Captain Vancouver's head to insert a light fixture, all four crew members signed their names on a sheet of paper and stuffed it inside the statue—or so the story goes. In the late 1970s, when the statue was brought down for regilding, no trace of the paper was found.

CHATHAM

HERALD ST

FISGARD S

PANDORA

JOHNSON

YATES ST.

WHARF ST.

FORT ST.

BROUGHT

COURTNE

HUMBOLD

Inner
Harbour

BELLEVILLE S

SUPERIOR S

MICHIGAN S

TORONTO ST

SIMCOE ST.

⌘ In this view from the Legislative Buildings around 1904–6, the Enterprise Wharf and, above it, the square Customs House (now the Malahat Building) are clearly visible. Following Wharf Street across the centre of the picture, we come to the old post office on the corner of Government Street. On the opposite side of Government is the old Belmont Saloon, with Weiler Brothers Home Furnishings behind it. Beside the saloon, houses and businesses still line Humboldt Street, with the towers of the Driard Hotel (now part of the Bay Centre) visible in the distance above them. In the right foreground, the Upper Causeway has been completed, and the waters of James Bay have been drained out from behind it, but the area that will become the grounds of the Empress Hotel is yet to be filled in. OPPOSITE View of the Inner Harbour from the Legislative Buildings in 2012.

CHATHAM

HERALD S

FISGARD :

PANDOR

JOHNSON

YATES ST.

WHARF ST.

FORT ST

BROUGHT

COURTN

HUMBOLD

Inner
Harbour

BELLEVILLE :

SUPERIOR :

MICHIGAN S

TORONTO ST

SIMCOE ST.

⌘ Looking along the causeway from the corner of Government and Belleville, we see the old post office still dominating the Wharf Street corner. There is no sign yet of the Imperial Oil gas station (now the Visitor Centre). Cars still drive on the left. The Belmont Building stands on the corner of Government and Humboldt, the time-ball mechanism on its roof clearly visible. On the right is the Empress Hotel, its original entrance roadway—where the Emily Carr statue is today—curving out of sight to the porte cochère. Today the view is much the same, but the traffic flow is greater, the post office has been replaced by a modern government building and the Belmont Building's time-ball mechanism has been made obsolete by wrist-watches and iPhones.

HENRY HUNT'S KWAKIUTL BEAR POLE

Northwest corner of
Belleville and Government

Kwakiutl (Kwakwaka'wakw) master carver Henry Hunt's cedar Bear Pole, often with a lone bagpiper in attendance during the warm weather months, has stood at the south end of the Upper Causeway since 1966. Poles display carved figures representing animals, ancestors or supernatural beings; they serve as markers of hereditary rights and privileges.

On this pole, reading from the top, we see the powerful Bear with Frog between his ears. Bear holds a copper in his mouth and paws, and beneath Bear is a Hamatsa dancer, wearing the ceremonial red cedar bark head and neck rings.

It is considered an honour to carve a story pole. Native carvers learn the craft at an early age, with carving techniques passed down from generation to generation. Four of Henry Hunt's sons have continued in their late father's tradition, becoming distinguished artists and carvers in their own right. Their work is featured at the Royal BC Museum and in Thunderbird Park.

⌘ Henry Hunt's Bear Pole, a hand-carved reminder of our peaceable First Nations, stands near the Peace Tulip Garden. Like the tall, square carillon in front of the Royal BC Museum (see page 108), this garden is dedicated to Canadians who helped liberate the Netherlands at the end of the Second World War.

CHATHAM
HERALD S
FISGARD
PANDOR
JOHNSON
YATES ST
WHARF ST.
FORT ST
BROUGHT
COURTN
HUMBOLD
Inner Harbour
BELLEVILLE
SUPERIOR
MICHIGAN S
TORONTO ST
SIMCOE ST.

⌘ Flowers along the grassy Belleville Street bank form a colourful accompaniment to the lone piper standing near Henry Hunt's Bear Pole.

PLAQUE COMMEMORATING THE ARRIVAL OF THE FIRST GROUP OF BLACK SETTLERS
South end of Upper Causeway wall

Sixty bronze plaques set in the wall of Victoria's Inner Harbour Causeway honour ships, companies, groups and individuals who were part of the history of Victoria. The plaques were a project spearheaded by local historian James K. Nesbitt and organized by the Victoria Centennial Pioneer Committee to commemorate the city's 100th birthday in 1962. Early-day ships remembered include the SS *Beaver*, which brought James Douglas here in 1843; the famous full-rigged tea clipper *Thermopylae*, which traded between Victoria and Rangoon in the 1890s; and the "bride ship" *Tynemouth*, bursting with young, marriageable women bound for these shores in 1862.

The plaque closest to the Legislative Buildings has particular significance. It commemorates a group of people who were celebrating the certainty of a new life, a new beginning, in a land far away from where they were born.

It was spring 1858, and the small Hudson's Bay Company settlement around Fort Victoria was buzzing with unaccustomed activity. For 15 years the fur trade had been the main focus for the men who worked at the fort and on the surrounding farms. But now there was new excitement—rumours of a gold find on the mainland had been confirmed.

In San Francisco, men from all four corners of the continent gathered on street corners, in saloons and around the docks, eager to book a passage north. Meanwhile, in the Zion Methodist Episcopal Church, a group of black families wanting to escape the threat of persecution and slavery in the so-called free state of California were discussing an unexpected invitation that had come their way. Captain Nagle of the HBC's SS *Beaver* brought news that James Douglas, chief factor at Fort Victoria and governor of the mainland and Vancouver Island colonies, was prepared to offer them land and freedom under the British flag.

Douglas, who had been born in British Guiana, the son of a Scottish merchant and a Barbados-born "free coloured woman," knew what it meant to be different and was sympathetic to the situation of the blacks in California. He wanted to help them . . . and

hoped that, in return, they would help him maintain a more civilized atmosphere in the Vancouver Island colony while gold fever raged on the mainland.

Without more ado, the church group decided to travel with the gold seekers to Vancouver Island. A few days later, on April 25, 1858, the *Commodore* sailed into Victoria's harbour bearing around 400 white prospectors—and 35 black men. While the miners steamed across the Strait of Georgia (now part of the Salish Sea) to the mainland, the blacks stayed in Victoria, determined to prove their worth to Governor Douglas.

Despite a lukewarm welcome from the white community—Dean Edward Cridge was their only true supporter—the newcomers, soon joined by their families, sent such favourable reports to friends and relatives back in San Francisco that within a few years, Victoria's black community had grown to more than 250 people. Some of this hardworking group started successful retail enterprises and were politically active. Peter Lester and Mifflin Gibbs operated the first independent, non-HBC provisioning business downtown. Gibbs was the first black man elected to city council. Samuel Ringo's restaurant became a firm favourite with locals

and visitors alike. Members of the group formed the self-supported, all-volunteer Victoria Pioneer Rifle Company (also known as the African Rifles), farmed in Saanich, and settled on Salt Spring Island, making significant contributions at every level in their respective communities.

They were free but, unfortunately, not free from racial prejudice, and by 1870 most of our original black settlers had returned south. Those who didn't were eventually laid to rest. In local churchyards, simple stones mark the final resting places of those early arrivals. And on the Inner Harbour, a plaque set in the top of the causeway wall reminds us of the black pioneers who came here to look for what the rest of us take for granted—the freedom to be whoever we are.

⌘ ABOVE LEFT Plaques set into the top of the low wall along the Upper Causeway remind us of sailing ships, seafarers, adventurers, people seeking freedom and young women brought here in the early 1860s as potential brides for the single men of Victoria.

⌘ ABOVE RIGHT Derek and Patricia Freeborn's bronzed likeness of Captain James Cook, charts tucked beneath one arm, stands solidly on the Upper Causeway with his back to the sea he loved so well. During his 1778 voyage of discovery under the British flag, Cook landed at Nootka Sound, helping to expand the British Empire by laying claim to this island. But it was his midshipman, George Vancouver, returning to the west coast as captain of his own ship in 1792, who drew the first map of the island. Almost a century later, the Canadian Pacific Railway announced that the western terminus of its newly completed transcontinental line would be the village of Granville—which became "Vancouver," in honour of the long-ago navigator who, literally, put it on the map.

CHATHAM
HERALD S
FISGARD
PANDOR
JOHNSON
YATES S
WHARF ST.
FORT S
BROUGH
COURTN
HUMBOLD
Inner
Harbour

FAIRMONT EMPRESS HOTEL
721 Government Street

When it opened in 1908, the Empress was the latest addition to the Canadian Pacific Railway's chain of luxury hotels—and Victoria's pride and joy. Several additions were made to the original centre portion, and the hotel underwent two major renovations over the years as travellers' tastes changed. Today, its distinctive, chateau-style roof, ivy-covered frontage and panoramic views make it the most-photographed structure on Victoria's Inner Harbour.

Empress Hotel from Parliament Buildings, Victoria, B.C.

⌘ A likeness of Victoria-born author and artist Emily Carr, with her beloved pet monkey, Woo, on her shoulder and dog Billie at her side, stands at the Fairmont Empress Hotel's original entrance gates, opposite the Royal BC Museum. The statue is the work of Calgary sculptor Barbara Paterson, creator of the *Women Are Persons!* monuments (also known as *The Famous Five* monuments) in Calgary's Olympic Square and on Parliament Hill, Ottawa. *Our Emily* was unveiled here in 2010. (See Emily's story on page 124.)

Starting on Belleville Street, at the south end of the Upper Causeway, Government Street runs right across the James Bay peninsula to the waterfront at Dallas Road. Bounded on three sides by water and on one side by parkland, this area has its own distinctive flavour.

In 1843 the Hudson's Bay Company set aside 10 acres of the peninsula for farming. Within a few years this agricultural reserve had expanded to 160 acres. Eventually the HBC sold the land to former employee William Walter Sims. He named it "Bexley Farm," after his wife's birthplace in England. However, as often happened in those early days, some careless scribe wrote "Beckley" instead of "Bexley," and so it has remained. The farm included Holland Point and most of the land now known as the James Bay neighbourhood.

In 1850, James Douglas built a home on the south shore of James Bay. As the years went by, others joined him. Fort Victoria was gone. The fur trade, flattened in the frantic rush for gold, was all but finished, and the relative peace and tranquility of downtown Victoria had given way to construction, swirling dust and clattering cartwheels. Families who had lived near the fort began seeking a quieter, cleaner, more civilized environment. In 1859 construction of a bridge from the south end of Government Street across James Bay inspired many to move to the peaceful pine-tree-covered peninsula at the other end of the bridge.

Victoria's first residential area quickly became its most favoured. Anxious to stay within reasonable reach of downtown stores, schools and churches, well-to-do families were the first to build homes along a short, unpaved street—Birdcage Walk—that took its name from the popular description of the nearby colonial administration buildings. (Locals thought these wooden buildings, designed by Hermann Otto Tiedemann in the late 1850s and early 1860s, looked like a cross between a pagoda and a birdcage.) The rough street extended south for two blocks from what is now Belleville to Michigan. There, a path skirted farmland before continuing as Carr Street, which led to the waterfront at Dallas Road.

James Bay changed a great deal over the decades. In the early 1900s, the wooden James Bay Bridge was replaced by a stone-and-concrete causeway, which eased access to the factories, mills, docks, grain terminals and cold storage plants that were appearing along the waterfront around the Inner Harbour. Light industry changed the flavour of the peninsula, and many of the well-to-do moved to other areas of town.

Today, high-rises and houses cover the land that Walter Sims once farmed, but James Bay remains a special place with a history all its own. A walk along Government Street affords a glimpse into the lives of some of the people who lived on this peninsula when Victoria was young.

ROYAL BC MUSEUM
675 Belleville at Government

The Royal BC Museum has come a long way from its humble beginnings in a small room in one of the early government buildings known as the Birdcages. In 1890 it was officially opened as the Provincial Museum of Natural History, and an archives was created four years later. When the new legislature was completed in 1898, the museum moved into its west wing and stayed there for most of the next seven decades.

In 1967, in conjunction with Canada's centennial, a new home was built for the museum at the corner of Government and Belleville Streets. Two years later, a separate building was added to house the BC Archives, and in 1987 the museum received its "Royal" designation at a special ceremony attended by His Royal Highness the Duke of Edinburgh. In 2003 the two organizations combined to form the Royal BC Museum Corporation.

Victorians are justifiably proud of their museum. Without a doubt one of the finest institutions of its type, it houses the National Geographic Imax Theatre as well as artifacts, documents and specimens from British Columbia's natural and human history. Archives, exhibits and galleries tell important stories about British Columbia, providing a unique window on the province's past, present and future.

The museum property also includes Elliott Street Square, featuring Helmcken House and St. Ann's Schoolhouse; Thunderbird Park; and the Netherlands Centennial Carillon (see page 108).

Dr. John Helmcken, first surgeon at Fort Victoria, married Cecilia, James Douglas's oldest daughter. The house that Helmcken built for his family is one of the oldest homes in Victoria—and indeed in the whole of British Columbia—still standing on its original site.

St. Ann's Schoolhouse was both home and workplace for the first four Sisters of St. Ann, who came here from Lachine, Quebec, in 1858. The crude log cabin had only two rooms, separated by a partition, and a chimney. The sisters lived and taught in one room and cooked in the other until the cabin could be enlarged. The schoolhouse originally stood in the Humboldt Valley, where St. Ann's Academy is today. It was moved to the museum site in 1974.

Thunderbird Park was developed in 1941 to display poles from the museum's collection. Over the years, the poles were moved inside for safekeeping. Kwakwaka'wakw

master carver Mungo Martin and a team including Henry Hunt and sons Tony and Richard carved the replica poles displayed around Wawadit'la (Mungo Martin House), a traditional longhouse still in regular use.

An ambitious, comprehensive, long-term redevelopment of the entire site is underway to ensure that the Royal BC Museum remains British Columbia's leading cultural centre, a place where the province's identity, collective memory, history and heritage can be preserved and enjoyed by all.

Rock Bay

YATES S

WHARF ST.

Inner Harbour

BELLEVILLE

SUPERIOR S

MICHIGAN

TORONTO S

MARIFIELD

SIMCOE ST.

NIAGARA ST.

BATTERY ST.

NETHERLANDS CENTENNIAL CARILLON
Southeast corner of
Government and Belleville

A prominent fixture at the corner of Government and Belleville Streets is the Netherlands Centennial Carillon—king of all carillons in Canada and a concrete link to Victoria's past. It is near the former location of "The Poplars," home of David Spencer, who developed Spencer's Arcade, Victoria's first Government Street department store, in the 1880s (it was located where the Bay Centre is today).

Today the carillon stands as evidence of a special connection between Canada and Holland. Carillons originated there in the mid-17th century as an adjunct to the Dutch tower-clock, announcing the time at frequent intervals with pleasing melodies and providing hand-played open-air music on festive occasions.

Unlike church bells, which move in response to the tug of bell-ringers' ropes, creating a sound when they hit the clapper (or when the clapper hits them), carillon bells are stationary. They don't move when rung, and the carilloneur doesn't physically touch them while playing. The bells are arranged in chromatic sequence and are actually played much like the strings on a piano. But there the similarity ends.

Carillon bells are struck by a series of clappers connected to wires that are, in turn, connected to a special keyboard located in a small cabin directly below them. This keyboard, known as a clavier, is made up of a series of wooden batons arranged in a row. A pianist uses a delicate touch to depress the piano keys. A carilloneur uses loosely closed fists to strike the batons, which pull the wires that cause the clappers to strike the bells.

Each baton's weight is determined by the size of the bell it's attached to; the heavier the bell, the more force is required to play it. The heaviest bells have batons that are played with the feet. There's no room for mistakes—once a bell has been struck, there's no way to alter or silence the sound. And the carilloneur must be able to use both hands and feet at the same time, while knowing the correct amount of force required for each bell. It's a specialized occupation, which explains why there are just a few carilloneurs in the whole of Canada.

Herman Bergink, who emigrated to Canada from the Netherlands in 1957 and was a founding member of the Dutch Canadian Centennial Committee, spearheaded the fundraising drive that made Victoria's carillon a reality. In 1967, Canada's Centennial year, Queen Juliana of the Netherlands laid the cornerstone, presenting the tower and the carillon to Victoria as a gift in recognition of Canada's role in the liberation of the Netherlands during the Second World War.

The provincial government designed and built the structure, which was completed and officially opened in May 1968 with 49 bells cast by Petit & Fritsen at the Royal Bell Foundry at Aarie-Rixtel, in Holland. By 1971 there were 62 bells, making Victoria's carillon the largest in Canada. Several bells are dedicated to landmarks in Victoria's history. The largest, called the bourdon, weighs around 1,500 kilograms and is dedicated to the centennial of the formation of the Crown Colony of Vancouver Island (1849–1949). Others are dedicated to the centennial of the establishment of the Crown Colony of BC (1858–1958); the centennial of BC joining Canadian Confederation (1871–1971); and the Canadian soldiers who gave their lives during the liberation of the Netherlands in the Second World War (1940–45).

When Herman Bergink retired in 1992, Dr. Rosemary Laing took over as provincial carilloneur. She climbs the carillon's spiral

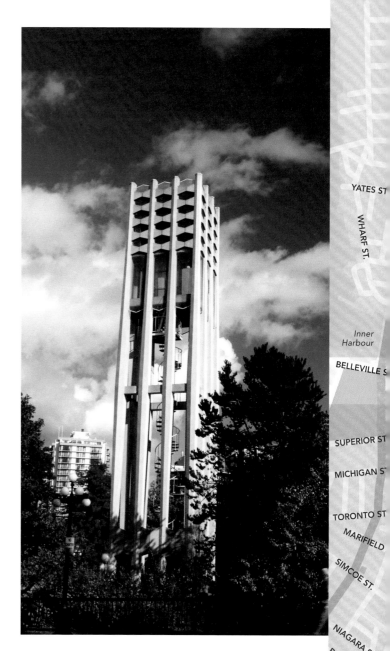

staircase—72 steps—to perform live recitals from her wide-ranging repertoire, which includes everything from classical music and folk songs to popular tunes. The joyous peal of the carillon's bells fills the air on summer weekends. And in August, the carillon bells join thundering cannons and fireworks in the closing moments of the *1812 Overture*, the traditional grand finale to Victoria's annual water-based extravaganza, Symphony Splash.

DOUGLAS AND HELMCKEN HOME SITES
Government and Belleville

Few corners in downtown Victoria contain as much history as the site where the Royal BC Museum now stands.

The first resident on the museum site was James Douglas, chief factor at the Hudson's Bay Company fort. Douglas, who in 1842 had chosen the site for Fort Victoria before returning to his post at Fort Vancouver on the Columbia River, moved to Fort Victoria permanently in 1849. He and his wife, Amelia, lived with their children in the chief factor's residence, just inside the fort's back gate.

In 1851, Douglas purchased an acreage bounded by what are now Belleville, Government, Superior and Douglas Streets, and had a new home built for his still-growing family. The house overlooked James Bay (which had been named after him), and the location was carefully chosen—far enough from the fort to afford some privacy, yet near enough for relatively easy access via the waterfront route that curved around James Bay's eastern end.

⌘ This plaque near the museum's back wall proclaims James Douglas's presence among us, and in particular the former location of his home. The marker stands near the scion of a cherry tree, now protected by an iron railing, that once stood in Douglas's orchard.

110

Douglas had come a long way from his beginnings, some 50 years earlier, in British Guiana (now Guyana). The son of a Scottish merchant and his Creole mistress, Douglas was schooled in Scotland before sailing, at the age of 16, to Montreal to join the fur trade. Journeying west, he crossed the Rockies into what was then known as New Caledonia.

At Fort St. James, on Stuart Lake, he met the woman who became his wife—Amelia, the mixed-blood daughter of Chief Factor William Connolly. There being no clergymen in those remote regions, Amelia and James were at first married "in the custom of the country"—the equivalent of a common-law marriage today—in 1828. Thirteen children were born to the couple over the next 25 years. Unfortunately, only six survived to adulthood.

After living in sparse, often shared, accommodations at various fur-trading posts, the Douglases were delighted with their first private, completely separate abode on Victoria's Inner Harbour. Their two-storey mansion boasted dormer windows facing north toward the fort, and gardens that sloped down to the waterfront. A fruit orchard flourished on the south side of "James Bay House." On the east side, a white picket fence separated the Douglases from their eldest daughter, Cecilia, who in 1852 had married Dr. John Sebastian Helmcken and lived next door at "Arbutus Lodge."

Douglas, now governor of Vancouver Island, enjoyed both his new status and his new home. He lived there through the Fraser River and Cariboo gold rushes, watched while the colonial administration buildings—known as the Birdcages—took shape on a neighbouring grassy slope, oversaw the demolition of Fort Victoria and witnessed the creation of the combined colonies of British Columbia. Honoured with a knighthood, bestowed by Queen Victoria in 1864, he eventually enjoyed a well-earned retirement until his death, at the age of 74, in 1877.

"Arbutus Lodge" (now called Helmcken House) still stands in Elliott Street Square behind the museum, but the Douglas home is gone, torn down in 1906 after Amelia Douglas died. A cairn behind the museum, and the scion of a cherry tree that once flowered in James Douglas's orchard, are all that's left to remind us of the first European to call this corner home.

⌘ LEFT Tucked away behind the museum in historic Elliott Street Square is a life-sized statue of Dr. John S. Helmcken, first surgeon at Fort Victoria, husband of James and Amelia Douglas's oldest daughter, Cecilia, and a statesman who helped negotiate BC's entry into Canada. His house is one of the oldest still standing in British Columbia and is open to visitors. The statue, which shows the good doctor leaving on some mission of mercy, stethoscope in one hand, medical bag in the other, was created by local artist Armando Barbon, who was born and trained in Italy. A short distance away, at Ogden Point, Barbon's likeness of Victoria town crier Tommy Mayne greets cruise ship passengers arriving at the terminal.

⌘ RIGHT Sunshine Coast sculptor Jack Harman's *Family Group* has intrigued museum visitors since the late 1960s. Examples of Harman's work, featured in Vancouver and nationwide, include *Miracle Mile* at the PNE grounds in Vancouver, the National Peacekeepers Memorial in Ottawa and an equestrian statue of Queen Elizabeth II on Parliament Hill in Ottawa.

QUEEN'S PRINTER
563 Superior at Government

The southwest corner of Government and Superior is dominated by a building that owes its presence to the nearby legislature. The Queen's Printer's history dates back to 1859, when Colonel Richard C. Moody of the Royal Engineers founded the capital of the Colony of British Columbia at Queensborough (later renamed New Westminster).

Two years after the mainland and Vancouver Island colonies were united in 1866 to become British Columbia, Victoria became the new capital. Richard Wolfenden, a lieutenant-colonel in the Royal Engineers,

⌘ In 1928 the King's Printer (now Queen's Printer) moved into this Art Deco-style building at the corner of Government and Superior Streets. Always busy with a variety of design and printing services, the Queen's Printer prepares documents to be read in the provincial legislature across the street and publishes the weekly *British Columbia Gazette*. In the elegant original foyer, you'll find a fascinating display of early printing equipment that was state-of-the-art when Queen Victoria was alive.

was appointed Queen's Printer. His department was located in one of the wooden administration buildings, fondly known as the Birdcages, which had stood on the Inner Harbour's south shore since 1859.

Rock Bay

YATES ST

WHARF ST.

Inner Harbour

BELLEVILLE S

SUPERIOR ST

MICHIGAN S

TORONTO ST

MARIFIELD

SIMCOE ST.

NIAGARA ST.

BATTERY ST.

By 1898 a new, stone legislature had been built on the same site. The printing department was located in its west wing. Three years later, when Queen Victoria died and was succeeded by her son, King Edward VII, Wolfenden became King's Printer. In 1903 he was created Western Canada's first Companion of the Imperial Service Order in recognition of his long and illustrious service.

The increasing demand for government printing services necessitated a move to more spacious quarters in 1928. New cement-built premises quickly took shape on a corner site behind the Parliament Buildings, with Saanich-born Charles Banfield at the helm. The first floor housed hand-fed printing presses. Printing and government office supplies were located on the second floor, while the third floor was home to the bindery.

Charles Banfield died in 1959, but *The British Columbia Gazette*, which he started, publishes weekly to this day. It includes notices to creditors, name changes, company registrations, notice of incorporations, amalgamations, dissolutions, public tenders and selected orders-in-council. Much of this information is also available online.

In 1989 the Superior Street building—which became the Queen's Printer once again in 1952—underwent major renovations. The main floor of the building features a fascinating display of printing equipment, once considered state-of-the-art but now classed as antique. The printing department employs more people than it did in Banfield's day, and the equipment they work with is many times more sophisticated, but he would be proud to know that they provide the same services he supervised there many decades ago.

FORMER ROBSON AND HUNTER HOMES
506 and 514 Government

In the mid-1800s, John Robson, soon to be the BC premier, made his home close to the colonial administration buildings, where he spent so much of his time. Purchasing property on the west side of what was then Birdcage Walk, Robson had two identical houses built. The one on the right—Number 514—was destined to be the home of Robson's daughter, Frances (Fanny) Hunter. Fanny's husband, Joseph, was a Scottish-born engineer who conducted surveys for the Canadian National Railroad and was responsible for surveying the Alaska–BC border. He later became a member of the legislative assembly.

John Robson and his wife, Susan, lived next door, at Number 506. Robson had arrived on the West Coast from Ontario in 1858, the year the Fraser River gold rush started. He settled in Queensborough (now New Westminster) and established the *British Columbian* newspaper. Thus began a bitter rivalry between Robson and Amor De Cosmos, editor of Victoria's *British Daily Colonist* (see the De Cosmos story on page 43), which continued when the two both became involved in provincial politics.

Robson moved to Victoria in 1869 after he was elected to the legislative assembly.

⌘ Just beyond the 1928 Queen's Printer building on Government Street's west side are two houses built by premier John Robson in 1885—one for his daughter, Fanny Hunter (No. 514), and one for himself (No. 506). In recent years, the beautifully restored Hunter house was home to the Crown Bookstore. In 2012, both houses, which have been owned by the provincial government since 1945, were empty.

When he became British Columbia's premier in 1889, his Birdcage Walk home was the setting for many social functions. He was only 68 and still premier when he died in 1892, the victim of blood poisoning that developed after he injured his finger.

Rock Bay

YATES ST.

WHARF ST.

Inner Harbour

BELLEVILLE S

SUPERIOR ST.

MICHIGAN ST

TORONTO ST.

MARIFIELD

SIMCOE ST.

NIAGARA ST.

BATTERY ST.

⌘ Corner stores make for nostalgic memories, and the Bird Cages Confectionery on the northeast corner of Government and Michigan is no exception. It takes us back to 1915, when Kleanthes (Pete) Metro erected this tiny store and moved his family into the house next door. Pete was manager of the Maryland Café, neighbour to W. & J. Wilson Clothiers in the 1200-block of Government Street. He died in 1927, but his wife, Orsa, and the children lived on at 503 Government until 1964. Government offices and high-rise apartments have replaced many of the lovely older homes in this area, and supermarkets have taken their toll, but the Bird Cages Confectionery, its colourful display of fragrant flowers perfuming the sidewalk, has survived. Take a look inside. Like many corner stores, this one is deceptive—its small interior is still big enough to hold everything the grocery shopper might need, and the current owner, who has had the store for more than three decades, lives next door at No. 503, just as the Metro family did all those years ago.

JAMES BAY INN
270 Government

James Bay is home to many bed and breakfast establishments and several other hotels. But because of its connection with the famous artist who once lived nearby, the James Bay Inn, at the corner of Government and Toronto Streets, stands out from them all.

When author and artist Emily Carr was born in 1871, James Bay was still the preferred place of residence for Victoria's elite. Separated by a wooden bridge from the dirt roads of downtown, it maintained an air of quiet gentility. However, by the time the James Bay Bridge was replaced by a concrete causeway 30 years later,

⌘ Built on a corner of the former Beckley Farm, the James Bay Inn is the third-oldest hostelry still in operation in Victoria. Owned by the same family for several decades, its interesting features—for example, no two rooms are alike—and friendly service have made it a favourite with residents and visitors alike.

most of James Bay's well-to-do residents had moved on. Government Street now extended from the Inner Harbour right through to Dallas Road, and James Bay became a favoured destination for visitors who, finding downtown hotels expensive, were looking for a moderately priced hostelry.

Designed by Victoria-born architect Charles Elwood Watkins and built by the Cornwall-born Parfitt brothers, the James Bay Hotel was completed in 1912. A double staircase led up from the street to the hotel's second-floor entrance, which faced Avalon Road and Beacon Hill Park. Visitors were impressed by the red Spanish-tile roof and spacious rooms, but less impressed by its location—the hotel was not, as

its name implied, on the bay, but in the middle of a residential community. So briefly, in the 1960s, it became the Colonial Inn, and its restaurant still carries that name.

The hotel has changed hands several times over the years. In 1942 it was bought by a Benedictine order and turned into St. Mary's Priory Guest House. Through what remained of the Second World War, the nursing sisters cared for residents and returning veterans. And it was here, less than a block from the house where she was born, that Emily Carr spent her final days.

Rock Bay

YATES ST.

WHARF ST.

Inner Harbour

BELLEVILLE S

SUPERIOR ST.

MICHIGAN ST

TORONTO ST.

MARIFIELD

SIMCOE ST.

NIAGARA ST.

BATTERY ST.

AVALON ROAD

The street opposite the front entrance of the James Bay Inn bears the name of a house built here by a man who discovered gold on the Sooke River, many kilometres away.

The year was 1864, and the city of Victoria was barely two years old. In the spring, Governor James Douglas—now Sir James—retired, and in the fall, the last of old Fort Victoria's buildings bit the dust. But exciting as these events were, nothing stirred up

⌘ Looking up Avalon Road, opposite the James Bay Inn, it's easy to see why Peter Leech chose to build his home at the top of it, close to Beacon Hill Park. Today the street is lined with lovingly preserved heritage homes, most built during the 1890s—the last years of Peter Leech's life.

as much excitement as the announcement that gold had been discovered just north of Victoria, near a place called Sooke.

Members of the Vancouver Island Exploring Expedition, all former Royal Engineers, were searching along the Sooke River for seeds and botanical specimens. The leader of the group, Captain Robert Brown, branched off and headed for Cowichan. His assistant, Lieutenant Peter Leech, a Dublin-born engineer, astronomer and former Crimean War fighter, carried on up a tributary of the river. It was here that one of his men, a fellow called Foley, found the gold.

The news caused quite a stir in the little city to the south. Victorians were old hands at gold rushes, this being their third in half a dozen years. But unlike the California and Cariboo gold finds, this one was a lot closer to home, and by the end of August 1864, enough gold had been found to spark serious interest. The rough trail from Victoria to Sooke wasn't wide enough for a wagon, so prospectors sailed into Sooke Harbour with their packhorses and supplies, then made their way up to Leech Creek. By the fall there were 500 men digging for gold; a few months later there were 3,000.

Around $100,000 worth of gold was taken from the river in that first year. But despite Leech Creek's promise, the longed-for motherlode never did materialize. Huge boulders the size of houses made it impossible to access the gravel in the rocky creek bed, and there was no equipment to move them. Disappointed, most of the fortune seekers left for greener pastures.

Lieutenant Leech worked in northern British Columbia before coming back to Victoria in 1873 to wed Mary Macdonald, a Calcutta-born, Scottish-educated lass. The Leeches settled at the east end of present-day Avalon Road. Their large, wooden "Avalon Villa," as Leech named it, faced directly onto Beacon Hill Park, where grand old trees and frog ponds formed a fine playground for his small daughter, Fanny.

Mary Leech became the organist at Bishop Cridge's Reformed Episcopal Church and played for weddings all over town. Peter Leech worked for the HBC for a while before becoming Victoria's city engineer; then, in the early 1890s, he travelled to Bella Coola to lay out the first townsite there. Shortly after his return, Mary developed pneumonia and died at the age of 55. Her husband lived on at "Avalon Villa" with their daughter until his own death in June 1899.

Today at Leech Creek, the ghosts of those long-ago gold miners must be shaking their heads in disbelief. There is no evidence of their mining camp. The trail is overgrown. Even "Avalon Villa" has gone, replaced by an apartment building. A display at the Sooke Region Museum, and Avalon Road in James Bay, are all that's left of the dashing young lieutenant and the flash-in-the-pan gold find that immortalized his name.

MARIFIELD AVENUE

Close to the James Bay Inn, where Emily Carr died, a short cross street called Marifield Avenue commemorates another "Emily connection"—Bishop Edward Cridge.

Cridge, who was born in Devonshire, was working in London when he learned, in 1854, that the Hudson's Bay Company was seeking a chaplain for its southern Vancouver Island outpost. By the end of the year he had gathered up his new bride, Mary, and his treasured cello and set sail on the *Marquis of Bute*. Arriving in Victoria five months later, he immediately started holding religious services in the fort.

When Victoria District Church was built on Church Hill (now Burdett Avenue), Cridge became its first dean. His was a busy but peaceful existence until Sunday, April 25, 1858. That was when the first boatload of Fraser River-bound gold miners sailed into Victoria's harbour, and Cridge's sleepy little parish was never the same again. Before long, men outnumbered women by 100 to one. The arrival in 1862 of a boatload of single women—sent by the Emigration Society in England at Cridge's request—relieved the situation somewhat, but 20 years later men still outnumbered women and the city had became a hotbed of bawdy behavior.

Cridge was concerned, but by this time he had more pressing problems. He and his superior, Bishop Hills, disagreed over the tone of church services, and Cridge decided to leave the Church of England. In a heartwarming display of loyalty, most of his congregation followed him down Church Hill to the east end of the James Bay mud flats, where a new church quickly started to take shape. The first service at the Church of our Lord was held in January 1876, and the congregation voted to join the Reformed Episcopal Church, with Cridge as their bishop.

Cridge bought land in James Bay. His house, named "Marifield Cottage" for his wife, boasted Victoria's first tennis court and a freshwater well. On the west side of Government, Marifield Avenue—originally

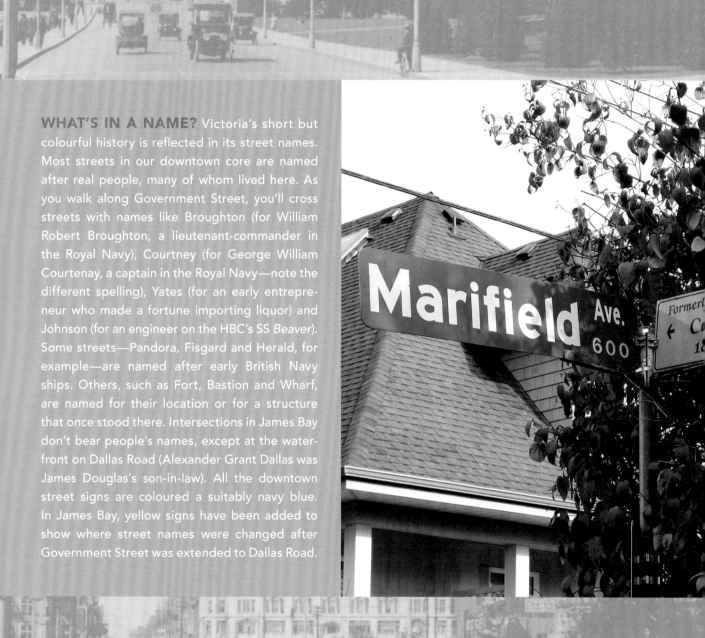

WHAT'S IN A NAME? Victoria's short but colourful history is reflected in its street names. Most streets in our downtown core are named after real people, many of whom lived here. As you walk along Government Street, you'll cross streets with names like Broughton (for William Robert Broughton, a lieutenant-commander in the Royal Navy), Courtney (for George William Courtenay, a captain in the Royal Navy—note the different spelling), Yates (for an early entrepreneur who made a fortune importing liquor) and Johnson (for an engineer on the HBC's SS *Beaver*). Some streets—Pandora, Fisgard and Herald, for example—are named after early British Navy ships. Others, such as Fort, Bastion and Wharf, are named for their location or for a structure that once stood there. Intersections in James Bay don't bear people's names, except at the waterfront on Dallas Road (Alexander Grant Dallas was James Douglas's son-in-law). All the downtown street signs are coloured a suitably navy blue. In James Bay, yellow signs have been added to show where street names were changed after Government Street was extended to Dallas Road.

⌘ Compare this view south along Government Street (formerly Carr Street) from Marifield Avenue in the early 1900s and the same view today, and it seems that little has changed apart from the difference in car and clothing fashions and the presence of overhead wires. Emily Carr's birthplace is in the distance, behind the trees on the left, just before the bend in the road.

CARR HOUSE
207 Government Street

Just four blocks away from where her Inner Harbour likeness fascinates passersby, Emily Carr's birthplace tells the story of Government Street's early days. Emily's father, Richard, had his house built on the west side of his four-acre property. It was here, on December 13, 1871, that Emily was born.

In the midst of the James Bay wilderness, Carr's corner of the world was as English as he could make it and uniquely his own. He preserved as many trees as possible, clearing the land between them for orchards and meadows. He built sheds for his cows, grew vegetables and planted several different kinds of bushes, vines and fruit trees. Then he enclosed his little empire with fences to keep his cows from wandering and his children in check.

Emily was the youngest of five girls. She was a bright, curious child with a passion for lilies and lilting prose. Flowers, animals and birds were a constant delight. Her best friends were the creatures in the cow-yard and Bong, the family's Chinese houseboy, all of whom seemed, unlike her siblings, to enjoy her loud, lusty singing.

called Cridge Avenue—led to the family home.

One day, while walking toward Dallas Road, Cridge met his young neighbour, Emily Carr. Anxious to show him her latest acquisition—a caged canary that she had been given as a birthday gift—Emily ran eagerly toward him and held up the cage for his inspection, but Cridge, deep in thought, ignored them both. Stung to the core, Emily never forgot that episode. Decades later, she recorded it in a collection of stories about her childhood called *The Book of Small*.

Emily would have been in her early 40s by the time Bishop Cridge died at "Marifield" in 1913 at the age of 96. Today, apartments have replaced the tall oaks and maples that once graced the Cridge property. But the short cul-de-sac called Marifield Avenue remains, a permanent reminder of the beloved chaplain who once ministered to the pioneers of this place.

When she was young, Emily sometimes walked with her father in the mornings along the rough road that led toward downtown. At today's Toronto Street, they took a dog-leg route around a cow farm, then followed Birdcage Walk to the south end of the wooden bridge that spanned James Bay (where the causeway is today). Here they would part, with Richard crossing the bridge to his provisioning business on Wharf Street and Emily making her way to school. We can almost see her pulling a wry face when her father bent down to kiss her goodbye.

Beacon Hill Park, which stretched along the eastern edge of the Carr property, was the setting for special times with her mother, whom Emily adored. They took picnics and sat on the grass, linking daisy chains in the

⌘ Emily's father Richard commissioned architects Wright & Sanders to design a home for his family. Constructed in 1863 of fir with California redwood trim, it contained every modern convenience, including a pump that brought water directly into the kitchen from a spring at the back of the house. In the days before Government Street was extended from Birdcage Walk to the Dallas Road waterfront, the road that ran by this house was called Carr Street.

peaceful silence. Long after her mother died, Emily returned again and again to the park to sketch, let her dogs run free, and revel in its timeless wild beauty.

Orphaned while still a teenager, Emily pleaded with her guardian to be allowed to follow her passion for painting and subsequently studied in California, London and

France. Her happiest times, however, were spent among First Nations people who recognized that, unlike others of her kind, Emily accepted and admired their ways. Over the years she journeyed through the wilderness of Vancouver Island and Haida Gwaii, living and painting in log cabins, tents, tool sheds, lighthouses and, eventually, a dilapidated old caravan that she called "The Elephant."

The recognition she longed for proved elusive, and she tried to support herself first as an art teacher, then as a landlady. In 1913 she built a house at 646 Simcoe Street, around the corner from the family home, that stands there to this day. She called it "The House of All Sorts," in reference to the tenants of all shapes, sizes and dispositions who came and went over the years. Intended as a source of revenue, the boarding house proved a miserable experience that stalled her painting career for more than a decade.

Finally, in the late 1920s, during a trip to Eastern Canada to see a display of her paintings at the National Gallery, Emily met the Group of Seven—artists famous for their depiction of Canadian landscapes. They declared her work "important." Thrilled to have their support, Emily was inspired to paint better than ever before, but the longed-for recognition and success stayed just beyond her reach.

On her 65th birthday, Emily feared that she was getting feeble and passé in her work. "I don't want to trickle out," she wrote. "I want to pour till the pail is empty, the last bit going out in a gush, not drops." Indeed, she went on to feature in solo exhibitions and took a writing course that resulted in several books about her life and times. The first, *Klee Wyck*, won a Governor General's Award. Then came *The Book of Small*. Other titles followed, their vivid, imaginative prose painting word-pictures of Emily's earlier days. But the constant struggle for acceptance of her abilities as an artist continued.

Eventually, ill health and deafness took their toll. Worn down by a series of heart attacks and strokes that would have felled a weaker woman, Emily eventually went into a nursing home (now the James Bay Inn) and died there in March 1945 at the age of 74. She could never have imagined that today her paintings would sell for more than $2 million, that her books would bring joy to all who read them or that her childhood home would become a national and provincial historic site.

Lovingly preserved, cared for and lived in since 1995 by curator Jan Ross and her family, Carr House is the jewel in James Bay's crown. More than just a museum, it's an interpretive centre—a place where you can explore and experience the life of one of Canada's national treasures, in the building where she was born.

WOODLANDS
140 Government Street

The big house behind the tall monkey-puzzle tree at 140 Government was the first to be built along the as-yet-unnamed road to the waterfront. James Bissett, who had been running the HBC's Hawaii office in Honolulu before his transfer here in 1860, bought five acres of land on the east side of Beckley Farm and had architects Wright & Sanders design his home. He called the Italianate Villa-style house, built in 1861, "Woodlands Cottage."

The Bissetts moved to Montreal in 1871 and rented the property to several families over the years. In the 1870s it was the home of Richard Wolfenden, then superintendent of printing in one of the Birdcage buildings (for the "Queen's Printer" story, see page 113). In 1889 the Bissetts sold the house to John Cowper Newbury, who had arrived in Victoria as a baby when his family moved here in 1863.

A bright boy from the start, Newbury was the first Victoria High School student to win the Governor General's medal for academic excellence. When he started teaching at Craigflower School (built in 1855 for the children of Craigflower Farm's Scottish community), Newbury was the youngest ever to hold the post. He later joined the Dominion Customs Service and moved with his parents and siblings to the former Bissett property in James Bay.

Newbury's property was bounded by Carr (later Government), Simcoe, South Turner and Niagara Streets. "Woodlands" faced onto Simcoe Street and was close to the home Richard Carr had built for his family in 1863. Newbury subdivided the land for his brother and sister and their families, and brought his now-widowed father to live with him at "Woodlands."

When Newbury married Emma Frye, he had "Woodlands" raised from the centre of the block and moved closer to Government Street. Thus the east side of the house became its front side, and Newbury hired well-known local architect Samuel Maclure to design a substantial addition at the south end.

The Newburys were a large and close-knit family. John's sister lived next door, at what is now 130 Government, and several uncles, aunts and cousins lived within a few blocks. John retired from the Customs Service in 1923 and died 11 years later. Emma died in 1963. Many Newbury descendants live in the Victoria area to this day—a very different city to the one John Newbury resided in over a century ago.

⌘ This fine Italianate Villa-style home was built in 1861, the year before Victoria was incorporated as a city and two years before Richard Carr's house was built nearby.

Government St.
near Dallas Rd.
Victoria B.C.

⌘ Looking north along tree-and-shrub-lined Government (formerly Carr) Street from close to Dallas Road in the early 1900s, we see family homes on both sides. Today the street is busier and the view from some of these homes has changed, but this section of Government Street remains almost as peaceful as when the first residents lived here, well over a century ago.

DALLAS ROAD

Government Street ends at Dallas Road, a winding waterfront route that stretches west and east as far as the eye can see, bordering the communities of James Bay and Fairfield, and continuing on as Beach Drive to Oak Bay and Cadboro Bay.

Dallas Road At some time or other, all of us have walked, biked or driven here. Interestingly, it is named not, as one might expect, for a city in Texas, but for Alexander Grant Dallas, who was sent here by the Hudson's Bay Company in 1857 to ensure that the company's best interests were being served by HBC chief factor and Vancouver Island governor James Douglas. The two men—one a lifelong fur trader, the other a successful international businessman and London-based HBC director—might have crossed swords had Dallas not cemented his success by marrying Jane, one of Douglas's pretty young daughters. When the Fraser River gold rush spurred the formation of the colony of British Columbia, Douglas transferred his allegiance to the Crown, and his son-in-law became head of the HBC's Western Department. Dallas and his family lived on Government Street. He left Victoria some years later, but our scenic waterfront still bears his name.

Holland Point Named for HBC employee George Holland, Holland Point was once part of Beckley Farm. Here, as elsewhere once Fort Victoria was established, fields traditionally used by the Lekwungen to grow camas and other native plants were appropriated for wheat, barley, oats, peas, potatoes and turnips—crops more appropriate to the newcomers' tastes. As wandering cattle and sheep ate the greenery, preventing the camas from flowering, and pigs rooted up the bulbs, all signs of Lekwungen agriculture disappeared. Today, Holland Point affords a view of the mountains on Washington State's Olympic Peninsula that is as spectacular today as it was to James Douglas and his men in the 1840s.

C.P.R. Tally-Ho Empress, Victoria, B.C.

⌘ After boarding the Empress Hotel's own special coach-and-six carriage at the Inner Harbour, these visitors would be treated to the same spectacular vista of Olympic Peninsula mountains that we enjoy today. A short distance east along Dallas Road from Government Street, at Mile Zero, is the monument to Terry Fox, who attempted to run across Canada to raise funds for cancer research. On the waterfront nearby, a sign shows where another young one-legged cancer victim, Steve Fonyo, completed the journey that Terry had been forced to abandon two years before, dipping his artificial leg into the cold waters of the Juan de Fuca Strait at Fonyo Beach.

Finlayson Point A short distance east, on the southern edge of Beacon Hill Park, is Finlayson Point. Centuries before James Douglas arrived, Holland and Finlayson Points were home to First Nations families and featured defensive fortifications. Roderick Finlayson, for whom the point is named, was a long-time Hudson's Bay Company employee who was posted to the newly established Fort Victoria in 1843 as second-in-command. The next year, after the unexpected death of his superior, he became chief factor. Finlayson later became first treasurer for the colonial government and, on retiring from the HBC, a successful businessman and respected politician. He was a member of the legislative assembly for many years and served as mayor of Victoria in 1878. The last surviving HBC man from the 1840s, his death in 1892 marked the end of an era.

Clover Point A little farther east along Dallas Road from Finlayson Point, Clover Point marks the spot where James Douglas first stepped ashore in 1842. Douglas and his men waded through knee-high clover, ferns and tall grasses in their search for a suitable spot to build a new fur-trading post. The arrival of white settlers spelled the beginning of the end for most native plant life. Today this bare, windy promontory is a firm favourite with outdoors enthusiasts including walkers, paragliders, windsurfers and kite flyers. Only its name reminds us that clover once grew on the waterfront at Clover Point.

Ogden Point West of Government along Dallas Road, a breakwater shields our cruise ship terminal and protects our harbour's inner reaches from fierce winter gales. Ogden Point is named for the HBC's Peter Skene Ogden. Hailing originally from Montreal, Ogden rose through HBC ranks and ended his working days at Fort St. James. Unlike Douglas, Finlayson and Dallas, Ogden never lived in Victoria and likely didn't even visit here. He died in Oregon City in 1854. A century and a half later, a breakwater pointed its long, double-jointed finger west across the Outer Harbour. A major construction feat involving 10,000 granite blocks stacked in a nine-layer pyramid, it was topped by a walkway that is still enjoyed by all who approach it from the point of land that bears Peter Skene Ogden's name. •

ient Street (East Side),
Victoria, B.C.

Government Street INTERESTING FACTS

- Fort Victoria was the first European settlement on Vancouver Island.

- Early British settlers sailed into our harbour around what they called Laurel Point. In fact, the vegetation was not laurel but salal.

- More than 2,500 bricks in Government Street's sidewalk mark the outline of Fort Victoria.

- Victoria is the oldest city in Western Canada.

- Victoria has more original heritage buildings still standing than any other city in Western Canada.

- During his 1792–94 exploration of this coast, Captain George Vancouver was the first to map the outline of Vancouver Island.

- The part of Government Street where Carr House stands was originally called Carr Street after Richard Carr donated land to the city for a road.

- Government Street was the first paved street west of the Rockies.

- The explosion in George Richardson's Windsor Hotel knocked down a couple of lamp standards on Government Street and could be heard clear out to Oak Bay.

- Robert Service, bard of the Yukon, was once employed by the Bank of British Columbia, at the corner of Government and Fort.

- Victorians drove on the left side of the road until December 31, 1921. Signs were changed overnight, and on the morning of January 1, 1922, everyone started driving on the right.

- Gas lighting appeared in the downtown business district in 1862.

- Waddington Alley was the first to feature wood-block paving. Soon, all Victoria's downtown streets were the same. The last wooden blocks were removed in 1948.

⌘ The arrival of the first boatload of Fraser River-bound gold miners in 1858 doubled Victoria's population in one day.

⌘ The Victoria townsite, laid out in 1852, was bounded by the harbour and today's Fort, Government and Johnson Streets. Ten years later, the eastern boundary was extended from Government Street to Douglas Street.

⌘ The queen after whom the city is named never visited Victoria—or, for that matter, much of the rest of her British Empire.

⌘ The first Sisters of St. Ann taught school in a wooden building near Beacon Hill Park that did double duty as their home until a proper school could be built.

⌘ Several islands in the harbour, as well as Laurel Point, were the sites of centuries-old Aboriginal gravesites.

⌘ The term "totem pole" originated among explorers, who assumed that First Nations peoples worshipped gods or idols. The correct name is Story Pole or Family Pole.

⌘ The city hall clock, installed in the clock tower in 1891, is still wound by hand once a week.

⌘ Charles "Candy" Rogers, who started making Rogers' Chocolates in 1885, was the first chocolatier in Canada. His first—and still the most popular—flavour? Vanilla Cream.

⌘ By the end of the 1800s, more than 95 percent of Canada's total Chinese population lived in Victoria's six-block Chinatown.

⌘ The Royal BC Museum houses over 2 million specimens, including woolly mammoth bones and First Nations cultural objects.

⌘ The unique sounds from the Netherlands Carillon are achieved when the carilloneur strikes clenched fists on the keyboard, causing attached levers to hit the bells.

⌘ Leading east from Government, Fort Street was the trail followed by First Nations people travelling to their village at Cadboro Bay.

⌘ Fort Victoria's bastions were 12-metre-high, 8-sided wooden towers containing 9-pounder cannons designed to protect the people at the fort.

⌘ Victoria's Chinatown, the oldest in Canada, is the second-oldest in North America. San Francisco's Chinatown dates from the 1849 California gold rush.

⌘ In Victoria, the manufacture and sale of opium was legal until 1908.

⌘ Victoria's city hall is the oldest such municipal building in British Columbia.

⌘ Look carefully at the Fairmont Empress and you'll see that the original (1908) centre block's bricks are slightly different than the ones used to build the south wing (1914) and the north wing (1925).

⌘ Built in 1874, the Customs House signified the end of the city's days as a free port.

Bibliography

Source material at the British Columbia Archives and Records Service and City of Victoria Archives was supplemented with information from the following books, as well as from Victoria's *Times Colonist* and newspapers of the News Group.

Camas Historical Group. *Camas Chronicles of James Bay*. Victoria: Evergreen Press, 1978.

Carr, Emily. *The Book of Small*. Toronto: Irwin Publishing Inc., 1942.

City of Victoria. "Downtown Heritage Registry." Victoria: Author, 1996.

Fawcett, Edgar. *Reminiscences of Old Victoria*. Toronto: William Briggs, 1912.

Grant, Peter. *Victoria: A History In Photographs*. Vancouver: Altitude Publishing, 1995.

Green, Valerie. *No Ordinary People*. Victoria: Beach Holme Publishers, 1992.

Griffin, Robert, and Nancy Oke. *Feeding the Family: 100 years of food and drink in Victoria*. Victoria: Royal BC Museum, 2011.

Humphreys, Danda. *On The Street Where You Live*. Vol. 1, *Pioneer Pathways of Early Victoria*. Surrey, BC: Heritage House, 1999.

——. *On The Street Where You Live*. Vol. 2, *Victoria's Early Roads and Railways*. Surrey, BC: Heritage House, 2000.

——. *On The Street Where You Live*. Vol. 3, *Sailors, Solicitors and Stargazers of Early Victoria*. Surrey, BC: Heritage House, 2001.

——. *Building Victoria: Men, Myths and Mortar*. Surrey, BC: Heritage House, 2004.

Kilian, Crawford. *Go Do Some Great Thing: The Black Pioneers of British Columbia*. Vancouver: Douglas & McIntyre Ltd., 1978.

Kluckner, Michael. *Victoria: The Way It Was*. North Vancouver: Whitecap Books, 1986.

Lai, David Chuen-yan. *The Forbidden City within Victoria*. Victoria: Orca Books, 1991.

———. *A Brief Chronology of Chinese Canadian History: From Segregation to Integration*. Chinese Canadian History Project Council. Vancouver: Simon Fraser University, David See-Chai Lam Centre for International Communication, 2011.

Obee, Dave. "Making the News." Victoria: Victoria *Times Colonist*, 2008.

Oke, Nancy, and Robert Griffin. *Feeding the Family: 100 Years of Food and Drink in Victoria*. Victoria: Royal BC Museum, 2011.

Rayner, William. *British Columbia's Premiers in Profile*. Surrey, BC: Heritage House, 2000.

Segger, Martin, and Douglas Franklin. *Exploring Victoria's Architecture*. Victoria: Sono Nis Press, 1996.

Smith, Dorothy Blakey (ed.). *The Reminiscences of Doctor John Sebastian Helmcken*. Vancouver: UBC Press, 1975.

Tomaszewski, Monika. "The History of Market Square." Victoria: 1989. Report available at the Market Square website, www.marketsquare.ca/. Click on the "About Us" button and choose "History of Market Square."

Victoria Heritage Foundation for the City of Victoria. *This Old House: Victoria's Heritage Neighbourhoods*. Vol. 2, *James Bay*. Victoria: VHF, 2005.

Walbran, John T. *British Columbia Coast Names, Their Origin and Their History*. Revised ed. Vancouver: J.J. Douglas Ltd., 1971.

Ward, Robin. *Echoes of Empire: Victoria and Its Remarkable Buildings*. Madeira Park, BC: Harbour Publishing, 1996.

Index

Page numbers in italics refer to images and captions.

Photo Credits

DANDA HUMPHREYS

14, 18, 19 (lower), 20, 22, 24 (lower right), 29, 31 (lower), 40 (inset), 47, 50 (lower left), 52, 56 (left), 57, 59 (left), 62 (centre), 63 (both), 66 (left), 69, 73 (lower), 87 (left), 89, 93 (all), 98 (inset), 104 (left lower), 110, 112 (left), 115 (left), 118, 121 (inset), 122 (lower)

DOWNTOWN VICTORIA BUSINESS ASSOCIATION

27 (bottom), 31 (top), 37 (left), 55, 75 (left), 77 (right), 81 (inset), 92, 93 (top centre), 95, 104 (left centre), 139

JOHN AND GLENDA CHERAMY

11, 12, 14-15, 24 (lower left), 34-35, 40 (background), 42 (upper), 49 (lower), 57 (background), 66-67, 70-71, 73 (top), 77 (left), 80, 88 (left), 96, 98, 103 (lower), 121 (background), 122 (top), 128 (top), 130 (top), 132-3, 135, 136

JOHN WALLS

14, 16, 17, 19 top, 22 (inset), 24 (top), 27 (top), 33, 37 (right), 39, 42 (lower), 43, 45, 46, 49 (top), 50 (top and lower right), 53 (all), 54 (both), 56 (right), 58, 59 (second left, centre and right), 60, 62 (right, left), 68, 71 (inset), 75 (right), 76, 78 (both), 81 (large), 82 (both), 84 (both), 86, 87 (right), 88 (right), 90, 94 (all), 99 (both), 100, 102 (both), 103 (top), 104 (top left and right), 107, 109, 112 (right), 115 (right), 116 (both), 117, 124 (both), 127, 128 (lower), 130 (lower)

LEGISLATIVE ASSEMBLY OF BRITISH COLUMBIA

97

QUEEN'S PRINTER FOR BRITISH COLUMBIA

113

ROYAL BC MUSEUM

106

Acknowledgements

This book has been a real adventure, and I'm fortunate to have been accompanied along the way by several stalwart travelling companions.

John and Glenda Cheramy generously shared their time and their amazing collection of old Victoria postcards, which have allowed us to peek so perfectly into Victoria's past.

Thanks also to the following people and organizations for information and help: the Hallmark Heritage Society; Valda Stefani and Trevor Livelton at City of Victoria Archives; the University of Victoria "Victoria's Victoria" website; the Royal BC Museum; Bill Ramsbottom, Provincial Capital Commission; Mel Harris, Legislative Assembly of British Columbia; Dawson Brenner, Queen's Printer for British Columbia; Ken Kelly and Alison Gair, Downtown Victoria Business Association;

Leslie Campbell and David Broadland, *Focus* magazine; and Karen Jawl.

Such a treat to work with photographer John Walls, whose enthusiasm for this book knows no bounds and whose many fine photographs enliven its pages.

As always, thanks to Rodger Touchie at the Heritage Group for his encouragement and support; also Vivian Sinclair for her direction and patience, Jacqui Thomas for her fabulous design, Kate Scallion for her patience and editor Audrey McClellan for successfully steering me through this, the fifth book we have worked on together.

Finally, to my *Times Colonist*, *Focus* magazine and *Homes & Living* magazine readers, as well as all those who over the years have joined me on walking tours through our historic downtown, or plan to explore it soon—this one's for you.

About the Author

Originally from Cheshire in northwest England, Danda has lived in Canada since 1972. Working over the years as a writer, actor, broadcaster, publicist and presentation skills coach, she arrived in Victoria in 1996 and was fascinated by the city's short but colourful history. Her stories about the people remembered in our street names appeared in Victoria's *Times Colonist* for five years. This is Danda's fifth book about early Victoria. She writes for local magazines and is active year-round as a conference speaker and storyteller-guide, making presentations to groups and leading walking tours through Victoria's historic downtown. You can visit her online at www.dandahumphreys.com.